BOSTON AND THE CIVIL WAR

Hub of the Second Revolution

BARBARA F. BERENSON

Charleston · London
The History Press

Published by The History Press
Charleston, SC 29403
www.historypress.net

Copyright © 2014 by Barbara F. Berenson
All rights reserved

First published 2014

Front cover: A New Regiment of Massachusetts Volunteers Passing Faneuil Hall on Their Way to the War. This lithograph was published in *Harper's Weekly* on August 17, 1861. *Reprinted with the permission of Applewood Books, Publishers of America's Living Past, Carlisle, MA 01741.*

Back cover: Sixth Regiment Memorial: Marching Through Baltimore. This mural, created by Richard Andrew in 1931, is located outside the House of Representatives Chamber of the Massachusetts State House. *Courtesy of the Commonwealth of Massachusetts Art Commission.*

Manufactured in the United States

ISBN 978.1.60949.949.5

Library of Congress CIP data applied for.

Notice: The information in this book is true and complete to the best of our knowledge. It is offered without guarantee on the part of the author or The History Press. The author and The History Press disclaim all liability in connection with the use of this book.

All rights reserved. No part of this book may be reproduced or transmitted in any form whatsoever without prior written permission from the publisher except in the case of brief quotations embodied in critical articles and reviews.

To Rick, Daniel and Alice

Contents

Acknowledgments	7
Introduction	9
1. The Birth of Abolitionism	11
2. Firebrands of Liberty	25
3. Stark Mad Abolitionists	41
4. The Lexington of 1861	63
5. Touched with Fire	81
6. The Dawn of the Women's Rights Revolution	97
7. The Fighting Irish	115
8. Emancipation!	127
9. Black Soldiers and Citizens	143
10. A New Birth of Freedom	159
Notes	173
Bibliography	181
Index	187
About the Author	191

Acknowledgments

I owe thanks to many. I am grateful to The History Press for inviting me to write this book and to Katie Orlando and Will Collicott for seeing it through to publication. My husband, who has been my partner in all things since we met in college, provided constant encouragement and served as my most important sounding board and editor. I developed some of the arguments made in this book while working on programs with Jayne Gordon and Kathleen Barker at the Massachusetts Historical Society. The justices of the Massachusetts Supreme Judicial Court have supported my interests in history and public education.

The Freedom Trail Foundation published *Walking Tours of Civil War Boston: Hub of Abolitionism* in 2011 as a special project to commemorate the Civil War sesquicentennial. I owe special thanks to those who have sponsored and attended my many Civil War talks and walks. Their enthusiasm, insightful comments and challenging questions motivated my research. I also appreciate the excellent work of the National Park Service in sharing Boston's Civil War history with residents and visitors.

I benefitted from exceptional assistance from a talented group of high school and college students: Sam Miller-Smith researched Boston's black and Irish regiments; Daniel Benett sifted through the letters of the soldiers profiled in Chapter 5; Caitlin McCarey helped to identify and obtain many images; Lauren Reisig researched Abigail Williams May; Alice Berenson taught me about Lucy Stone and the postwar split in the woman's suffrage movement; and Jason Goodman optimized my final selection of digital images.

Acknowledgments

Many careful readers reviewed all or portions of my draft manuscript: Tom Ambrosino, Alice Berenson, Daniel Berenson, Richard Berenson, Kathleen Barker, David Brodsky, Richard Campagna, Carol Cohen, Jerome Fischbein, Elizabeth Fischbein, Laurence Golding, Jayne Gordon, Mona Hochberg, Kasey Kaufman, Jack Kavanaugh, Joan Kenney, Marc Laredo, Sandra Lundy, Roger Michel, Elizabeth Mulvey, John Paine, Gillian Pearson and Robin Tapper. Of course, any errors are mine alone. My family and friends provided marvelous support; I could not have completed this book without their encouragement and enthusiasm.

Many librarians were unfailingly helpful in tracking down information and images: Carole Doody at the Social Law Library; Peter Drummey and Anna Clutterbuck-Cook at the Massachusetts Historical Society; Tom Blake, Sean Casey and Jane Winton at the Boston Public Library; Patricia Boulos at the Boston Athenaeum; Susan Greendyke Lachevre at the Commonwealth of Massachusetts Art Commission; Leslie Schoenfeld at the Harvard Law School Library; Amy Burton at the Office of Senate Curator at the United States Senate; Michael Millner at the Carolina Digital Library and Archives; Lily Birkhimer at the Ohio Historical Society; and many helpful librarians at the Newton Free Library and throughout the Minuteman Library System.

Introduction

Most people know that the American Revolution began in Boston when a group of radical activists protested British governance of the colonies. But many people don't know that the nation's Civil War—the war that ended slavery—also began in Boston. Led by agitator and publisher William Lloyd Garrison, a group of radical abolitionists protested against Southern slavery and Northern acquiescence in the South's "peculiar institution."

Guided by the example of Revolutionary-era Patriots who persuasively argued for independence while organizing dramatic protests such as the Boston Tea Party, Boston's black and white activists organized an unrelenting campaign against slavery and racism. As the antislavery movement grew, Southern slaveholders became more determined than ever to resist any proposals that would limit the spread of slavery.

After Northerners elected Abraham Lincoln to the presidency in 1860, eleven Southern states seceded from the Union. When Lincoln went to war to restore the Union, Boston's abolitionists tirelessly campaigned for expanding the aims of war to include the permanent elimination of slavery. They led a Second American Revolution intended to force the nation to live up to the promises of liberty and equality contained in the Declaration of Independence.

In 2011, inspired by the sesquicentennial of the Civil War, I wrote *Walking Tours of Civil War Boston: Hub of Abolitionism* to share the important and fascinating story of Civil War Boston with residents and visitors. This book expands on that effort, narrating in substantially more detail the story of

Introduction

how Boston again altered the fate of the nation. Chapters 1 and 2 provide an introduction to the roots of Boston's abolitionism and its growth during the prewar years. Chapter 3 describes how the Fugitive Slave Act of 1850, which led to dramatic returns of runaway slaves from downtown Boston, was a turning point in the development of the antislavery movement. Chapter 4 addresses the immediate causes of war—highlighting their extensive Boston connections—and explains the significance of the "Lexington of 1861." In an astonishing historical coincidence, the first Union soldiers to die in combat were Massachusetts men killed on April 19, 1861—the anniversary of the 1775 battles of Lexington and Concord. Chapter 5 profiles the experiences of a select group of Boston's soldiers, while Chapter 6 sketches the contributions of prominent Boston women. Chapter 7 highlights the significant role of Boston's growing Irish community during the antebellum and war years. The final chapters focus on emancipation. Chapter 8 explains how Boston's abolitionists helped persuade Lincoln to issue the Emancipation Proclamation; Chapter 9 describes Boston's famous black regiments; and Chapter 10 addresses the leading role of Boston's abolitionists in the ultimately successful effort to amend the Constitution to permanently ban slavery throughout the nation.

Chapter 1

THE BIRTH OF ABOLITIONISM

"I am in earnest—I will not equivocate—I will not excuse—I will not retreat a single inch—AND I WILL BE HEARD." These words were emblazoned across the first issue of *The Liberator* newspaper, published in Boston on January 1, 1831. With them, William Lloyd Garrison inaugurated a national abolitionist movement dedicated to the immediate end of slavery. Garrison, a white man, welcomed blacks and women to join him in opposing oppression. His paper and the radical movement it spawned would lead directly and inexorably to the Civil War thirty years later.

Garrison, who hailed from the North Shore town of Newburyport, announced his determination "to lift up the standard of emancipation in the eyes of the nation, within sight of Bunker Hill and in the birthplace of liberty." The choice of Boston as his base was well made. While Garrison harshly criticized most Bostonians' indifference to slavery, the city's history of active abolitionism dated back to the Revolutionary era. Boston's white Patriots, free blacks and slaves had acted on the promises of freedom contained in the Declaration of Independence to make Massachusetts, in 1783, the first state in the new nation to abolish slavery.

BOSTON AND THE CIVIL WAR

SLAVERY IN MASSACHUSETTS

Ironically, Massachusetts was also the first colony to legally endorse slavery, incorporating it in 1641 into the paradoxically named Body of Liberties, the colony's first legal code. Yet voices early in the Revolutionary struggle would speak out against the practice. Patriot leader John Adams credited James Otis with initiating the movement for independence from Great Britain when Otis argued in 1761 that British writs of assistance, which allowed warrantless searches, violated "natural law," which gave every man the right to life and liberty. "Then and there," wrote Adams, "the child independence was born." Several years later, Otis called attention to the inconsistency of arguing for freedom for the American colonies while denying it to a class of persons living in their midst. "The Colonists are by the law of nature free born, as indeed all men are, white or black," he wrote.

When Otis published *The Rights of the British Colonies Asserted and Proved* in 1764, 2.2 percent of the inhabitants of Massachusetts were slaves. In coastal Boston, nearly 10 percent of the almost sixteen thousand residents were slaves. The largest slaveholding family, the Royalls of Medford, owned several dozen slaves. Though few Bostonians are aware of this aspect of their city's history, Boston's colonial-era newspapers advertised for the purchase and sale of slaves, and courts enforced contracts involving the sale of slaves.

Discussions over the future of slavery continued in Boston throughout the American Revolution. The legality of enslaving Africans was the subject of Harvard College's commencement debate in 1773, the same year as Boston's famous Tea Party. An unsuccessful attempt to outlaw the slave trade was made in 1774. That same year, local black poet and slave Phillis Wheatley wrote, "[I]n every human breast, God has implanted a principle, which we call love of freedom; it is impatient of oppression and pants for deliverance." Abigail Adams, an acute observer of Boston mores and morals, told John Adams, her husband, who was serving in the Continental Congress in Philadelphia, "I wish most sincerely there was not a slave in the province. It always appeared a most iniquitous scheme to me [to] fight ourselves for what we are daily robbing and plundering from those who have as good a right [to] freedom as we have."

Hub of the Second Revolution

The End of Slavery in Massachusetts

Demands for the end of slavery in Massachusetts increased following the colonies' adoption of the Declaration of Independence on July 4, 1776. Led by Prince Hall, a free black man, Boston's free and enslaved blacks organized a series of antislavery petitions to the Massachusetts legislature. The petition of January 1777, which relied on the soaring rhetoric of the Declaration of Independence, postulated that blacks enslaved in Massachusetts "have in common with all other men a natural and unalienable right" to freedom and alleged that every argument of the enslaved "pleads stronger than a thousand arguments" against Great Britain. The Massachusetts state constitution of 1780, drafted by John Adams and adopted while war with Great Britain raged, echoed the Declaration of Independence's promises of equality and liberty. Article I of the constitution proclaimed, "All men are born free and equal, and have certain natural, essential, and unalienable rights; among which may be reckoned the right of enjoying and defending their lives and liberties; that of acquiring, possessing, and protecting property; in fine, that of seeking and obtaining their safety and happiness."

Although the abolition of slavery was not a stated goal of Article I, some in Massachusetts saw a direct connection. In their votes to ratify the proposed constitution, delegates from several towns recommended explicitly outlawing slavery. The town of Hardwick proposed that Article I be revised to state, "[A]ll men, white and black, are born free and equal" so that it could not be "misconstrued hereafter in such a manner as to exclude blacks." Braintree, where the Adams family lived, also sought an explicit end to slavery, explaining that "when we have long struggled, at the expense of much treasure and blood, to obtain liberty for ourselves and posterity, it ill becomes us to enslave others who have an equal right to liberty with ourselves."[1]

Soon after the Massachusetts Constitution was adopted, two court cases brought by slaves with the assistance of white lawyers ended slavery in the young state. In 1781, a household slave known as Mum Bett sued for her freedom after hearing a public reading of the Declaration of Independence. With assistance from lawyer Theodore Sedgwick, Mum Bett prevailed in her case. A jury in western Massachusetts concluded that the Massachusetts Constitution had effectively outlawed slavery and fined the man who had claimed to own her thirty shillings. Mum Bett was thereafter known as Elizabeth Freeman. She worked for Theodore Sedgwick's family as a paid caretaker, and when she died, she was buried in a place of honor in the

Mum Bett, also known as Elizabeth Freeman. *Courtesy of the Massachusetts Historical Society.*

Sedgwick family plot. Sedgwick's advocacy did not diminish his legal stature; he later served as a U.S. representative, a U.S. senator and a justice of the Massachusetts Supreme Judicial Court.

Also in 1781, Quock Walker, a black slave in Worcester County, ran away. His owner's beating of Walker upon his recapture led to a series of lawsuits that challenged the authority of a "master" to beat his "property." Levi Lincoln, Walker's lawyer, argued, "Is it not a law of nature that all men are equal and free—Is not the law of nature the law of God—Is not the law of God, then, against slavery?" Garrison and other nineteenth-century abolitionists would later argue that a "higher" law of freedom took precedence over man-made laws codifying slavery.

William Cushing, the chief justice of the Supreme Judicial Court, instructed a Massachusetts jury hearing Walker's case that slavery was incompatible with the rights set forth in the recently adopted constitution of the Commonwealth of Massachusetts: "[Our constitution declares] that all men are born free and equal; and that every subject is entitled to liberty, and to have it guarded by the laws as well as his life and property. [S]lavery is in my judgment as effectively abolished as it can be by the granting of rights and privileges wholly incompatible and repugnant to its existence."

The jury found that Quock Walker's master lacked the authority to administer a beating. No Massachusetts slaveholder ever again attempted to assert a legal right to claim a person as property, and the 1790 census recorded no slaves in Massachusetts.

Slavery and the U.S. Constitution

In contrast to the soaring rhetoric of liberty and equality contained in the Declaration of Independence, the U.S. Constitution of 1787 explicitly permitted slavery, although the framers avoided using the term, aware that it would taint the nation's charter. For purposes of appointing representatives to the U.S. House of Representatives, those "bound to service" were counted as three-fifths of a free person, thus ensuring that white voters in states with large numbers of slaves would exert a disproportionate influence on national policy. The "importation of such persons as any of the states now admitted shall think proper to admit" (slave trade) was protected until at least 1808. Article IV provided for the return of one "held to service or labor" who had escaped to another state.

These clauses stemmed from the compromises necessary to create the Union, although some founders vehemently protested these concessions to slavery. Future generations would have to resolve the chasm between the Declaration of Independence's lofty promises and the Constitution's legal rules. They would also have to determine whether the Constitution was permanently destined to be a pro-slavery document or if the commitments articulated in the Preamble—to "form a more perfect Union" and "secure the Blessings of Liberty"—contained the seeds of emancipation. This would, of course, require the nation to define whether liberty meant the right of slave owners to their property or the right of all people to be free.

Boston and the Civil War

The Growth of a New Society

The morality of slavery receded as an interest of Boston's whites for several decades following the end of slavery in Massachusetts. Instead, concerns turned to local pocketbooks. Boston had taken a financial pounding during the Revolutionary War. When the British Trade Act of 1774 closed the port to all commerce, merchants shifted their business to other cities on the East Coast. Even after the peace treaty with Britain in 1783, the Port of Boston, which had been the economic engine of the city, regained traffic only slowly until the second decade of the nineteenth century.

After Francis Cabot Lowell opened the nation's first textile factory in 1814 in suburban Waltham, Boston's fortunes began to change. The city's early industrialists, children and grandchildren of the Revolutionary Patriots, made fortunes from factories that transformed Southern slave-grown cotton into cloth. Slavery helped power the economic engine behind Boston's resumed commercial success in manufacturing, banking, shipping, transportation and other industries. Close economic and social ties developed between those whom abolitionists would call the "lords of the loom" and the "lords of the lash." These ties would continue to grow every year into the 1850s.

The issue of slavery first threatened to disturb this relatively tranquil period of growth in 1820, when the slave state of Missouri petitioned for admission to the Union. Its admission would have undone the careful balance between slave and free states. By this time, other Northern states had passed laws providing for the gradual end of slavery, and slavery had become a purely Southern affair. The Compromise of 1820 maintained sectional balance by admitting Missouri as a slave state and Maine (which had been a part of Massachusetts) as a free state. Further emphasizing that slavery was now a peculiarly Southern institution, the Missouri Compromise also banned slavery in all territory that had been acquired in the Louisiana Purchase north of the latitude of 36° 30′. Americans hoped that the Missouri Compromise had "solved" the sectional disputes over slavery, and the issue again largely receded from public debate.

Awakenings

The religious revival movement known as the Second Great Awakening swept across the Northeast during the first decades of the nineteenth century.

Hub of the Second Revolution

(The First Great Awakening was a mid-eighteenth-century Christian revival movement.) Before subsiding in the 1840s, the Second Awakening spread like wildfire through different Protestant denominations and led to a massive growth in the Methodist and Baptist denominations among both whites and blacks. Mass revival meetings sprang up, led by reformers who preached that salvation required working toward the moral perfection of individuals and society. The ethos of the awakening helped spawn a variety of social reform movements, including those for abolitionism, temperance, school reform and women's rights.

Black churches were the center of Boston's small and close-knit black community; the number of blacks living in Boston remained under two thousand even as the white population grew to sixty-one thousand by 1830. More than half of Boston's blacks lived on the north slope of Beacon Hill. The First African Baptist Church, also known as the African Meeting House, opened on Beacon Hill in 1806, and a black Methodist church was established in 1818. The all-black African school (later renamed the Abiel Smith School) was initially located in the African Meeting House before moving to a building next door. Boston's blacks typically eked out a meager living in unskilled and menial jobs, although some owned small businesses that catered primarily to their own community. Laws or customs of the white majority guaranteed discriminatory treatment or segregation of blacks in most aspects of daily life.

In 1826, members of Boston's black community formed the Massachusetts General Colored Association to advocate for education and moral improvement and against racism and slavery. Among the association's founders was David Walker, a black man who had been born free in North Carolina around 1796 and lived in Charleston, South Carolina, and Philadelphia before coming to Boston in 1825. Walker established a small used-clothing business and served as a subscription agent for the first newspaper owned and operated by black Americans. *Freedom's Journal* was published weekly in New York City beginning in 1827, the same year slavery ended in New York State.[2]

In September 1829, Walker published his momentous *Appeal to the Coloured Citizens of the World*. He wrote in the preamble to the lengthy pamphlet, "We (coloured people of these United States) are the most degraded, wretched, and abject set of beings that ever lived since the world began." In four "articles" or essays based on his observations of black life in both Northern and Southern states, Walker described the miserable lives of both enslaved and free African Americans and argued that race-based slavery was the cause of Northern racial discrimination. He accused whites of ignoring the supposed self-evident truths of the Declaration of Independence and urged them to compare its language with the "cruelties and murders inflicted by your cruel and unmerciful fathers and yourselves on our father and on us." He also warned whites of the consequences if his words were not heeded: "And wo, wo, will be to you if we have to obtain our freedom by fighting."

Copies of Walker's *Appeal* traveled quickly throughout black communities across the nation even though enraged Southern slaveholders persuaded their state governments to ban it and impose harsh penalties on those possessing or circulating it. Demand was so high that Walker published three editions within a few months. Unfortunately, he died on August 6, 1830, likely of tuberculosis, although rumors abounded that pro-slavery sympathizers had murdered him.

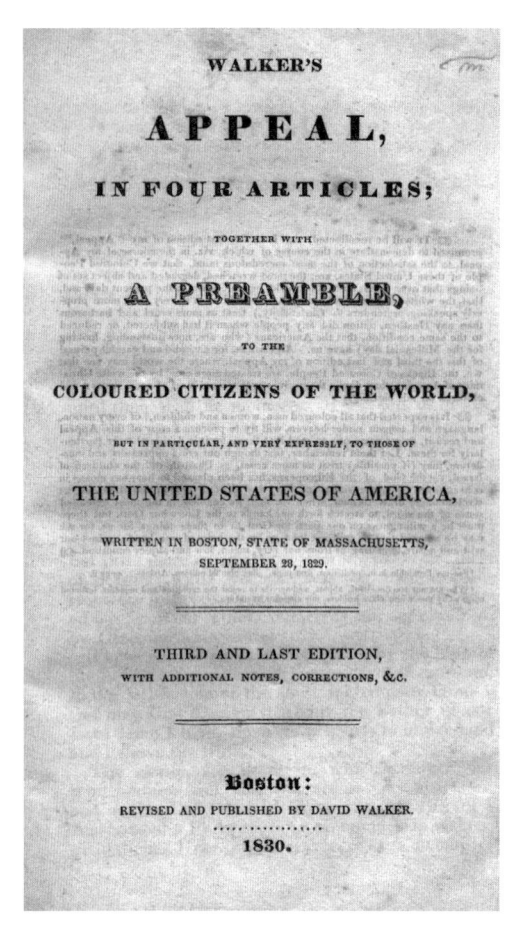

First page of David Walker's *Appeal to the Coloured Citizens of the World*. Courtesy of the University Library, University of North Carolina at Chapel Hill.

WILLIAM LLOYD GARRISON AND *THE LIBERATOR*

In the same year that Walker published his *Appeal*, William Lloyd Garrison came to Boston to deliver his first public antislavery speech. Garrison, who was born in Newburyport, Massachusetts, in 1805, had apprenticed at a newspaper in his hometown, where he honed his skills as both a debater and a printer. In 1828, he met Benjamin Lundy, a Quaker abolitionist and publisher of a Baltimore weekly called *The Genius of Universal Emancipation*. Lundy had organized an antislavery association in 1815 and started his newspaper in 1821. Many early abolitionists were Quakers, since slavery contravened the Quaker belief in the universal sanctity of life. Inspired by Lundy's hatred of slavery and sharing his pacifist views, Garrison joined him as assistant editor. In Baltimore, Garrison developed ties with local blacks that would prove critical when he later sought to forge relations in Boston's much smaller and close-knit black community.

The American Colonization Society invited Garrison, then twenty-four years old, to give an Independence Day speech at Boston's Park Street Church on July 4, 1829. The Colonization Society, which was founded in 1817, had acquired territory in West Africa, renamed it Liberia and raised money to resettle a small number of black Americans there. Supporters of colonization hoped to encourage slaveholders to gradually free slaves, who would then be transported to Africa. Many supporters of colonization also hoped to "repatriate" free blacks to Africa. The vast majority of Northern whites willing to acknowledge the immorality of slavery supported gradual emancipation accompanied by colonization, as they were unprepared to contemplate American society absorbing more than 2 million freed slaves. In his *Appeal*, Walker had strenuously criticized colonization as a trick of whites designed to permanently perpetuate the continuation of slavery and racism.

Garrison's speech at the Park Street Church minced no words in describing what he regarded as the founding hypocrisy of the United States: "Every Fourth of July, our Declaration of Independence is produced to set forth the tyranny of the mother country," he thundered. "But what a pitiful detail of grievances does this document present, in comparison with the wrongs which our slaves endure…[I]t is the sting of the wasp contrasted with the tortures of the Inquisition." In addition to attacking slavery in the South, Garrison harshly criticized what he regarded as the complicity of the North. The free states "are constitutionally involved in the guilt of slavery, by adhering to a national compact that sanctions it…and it is their duty to assist in its overthrow." He also took issue with those who proclaimed the natural inferiority of blacks, declaring "education and freedom will elevate our colored population to a rank with the white—making them useful, intelligent and peaceable citizens."

However, even Garrison was unable at that time to imagine the consequences for the nation if all slaves were immediately freed. He recommended a gradualist approach, stating that "[t]he fabric [of slavery]

Park Street Church, where William Lloyd Garrison delivered his 1829 speech. *Courtesy of the Boston Public Library.*

must be taken away brick by brick, and foot by foot, till it is reduced so low that it may be overturned without burying the nation in its ruins. Years may elapse before the completion of the achievement."

After his speech, Garrison returned to Baltimore, but he and Lundy soon amicably parted. Likely influenced by Walker's *Appeal*, Garrison now embraced immediate emancipation and opposed both colonization and gradualism. He also resolved to campaign for full civil and political equality for blacks.

Garrison considered possible locations to start his own antislavery weekly newspaper. Boston was an obvious choice. In addition to his personal ties to Massachusetts, Garrison had determined to "follow the revolutionary path of [John] Adams and [James] Otis and inspire a moral reformation in the shadow of Faneuil Hall."[3] Boston, which would be nicknamed the "Hub" in 1858, was also the nation's leading intellectual center.

Garrison promptly sought alliances within Boston's black community. He reached out to Reverend Samuel Snowden, an outspoken opponent of slavery at whose Methodist church David Walker had worshipped, and to Reverend Thomas Paul, the pastor of the African Baptist Church. They in turn introduced Garrison to other members of Boston's black community. Garrison also found a handful of local white supporters, including lawyer Samuel E. Sewall and his cousin, Connecticut Unitarian minister Samuel Joseph May. Their ancestor, Samuel Sewall, had presided over the Salem witch trials in 1692 but later apologized for his role and wrote *The Selling of Joseph*, the first antislavery tract published in North America.

On January 1, 1831, Garrison published the first issue of *The Liberator*. Within "sight of Bunker Hill and in the birthplace of liberty," he announced that his goals were immediate emancipation of all slaves and full legal equality for all blacks, including those currently enslaved. Garrison promised:

> *I will be as harsh as truth, and as uncompromising as justice. On this subject, I do not wish to think, or speak, or write, with moderation. No! no! Tell a man whose house is on fire, to give a moderate alarm; tell him to moderately rescue his wife from the hand of the ravisher; tell the mother to gradually extricate her babe from the fire into which it has fallen; but urge me not to use moderation in a cause like the present. I am in earnest—I will not equivocate—I will not excuse—I will not retreat a single inch—AND I WILL BE HEARD.*

In the first issues of his weekly paper, Garrison repeatedly called attention to Walker's *Appeal* despite noting his disagreement with its

William Lloyd Garrison with an early edition of *The Liberator*. *Courtesy of the Boston Public Library.*

endorsement of violence. Garrison thereby introduced a long-standing strategic accommodation in Boston's abolitionist movement. Although Garrison personally favored moral suasion and eschewed violent tactics, *The Liberator* would publish and promote the antislavery writings of those who advocated insurrection and violence.

During *The Liberator*'s first years, black subscribers kept the publication afloat. In 1831, fewer than 50 of its 450 subscribers were white. Garrison and Isaac Knapp, a childhood friend who initially served as co-publisher, were so poor that they slept on a mattress in the corner of the small office.

Garrison, who intended to foment a full egalitarian crusade, enthusiastically invited women to write for *The Liberator* and participate in the abolitionist movement. Significant early female allies included Maria Stewart, a black woman who defied a long-standing custom that prohibited women from speaking publicly on political issues, and Lydia Maria Child, a white woman who wrote the first book-length antislavery tract. (The short path from public activism against slavery to campaigning for women's rights is discussed in Chapter 6, which includes brief profiles of Stewart and Child.)

Garrison harshly accused the framers of the U.S. Constitution of trampling the Declaration of Independence beneath their feet as they placated Southern slaveholders. Although he did not yet explicitly call for "disunion" or separation of the North from the South, he presciently predicted that the continuation of slavery would, if left alone, "very speedily destroy this Union." Garrison counseled that preserving a Union with slavery is "not worth a price like this…Let the pillars thereof fall—let the superstructure crumble into dust—if it must be upheld by robbery and oppression."

Daniel Webster and the Supremacy of Union

Among white Bostonians in 1831, Garrison's was a voice in the wilderness. Few whites were prepared to heed his claim that their nation was founded on hypocrisy. Even those who agreed that slavery was a moral evil were generally prepared to support the status quo and assuage their misgivings by endorsing the colonization movement. Above all, white Boston was loyal to the Constitution and the Union it created. U.S. senator Daniel Webster, who personally found slavery odious, was the state's—and the North's—leading spokesman for the superiority of the American Union and its system of free and popular government. Webster was a brilliant lawyer and orator whose thrilling phrases, spellbinding delivery and dramatic looks had earned him the moniker "Godlike Daniel."

In the U.S. Senate, Webster famously championed the preeminence of the Union in response to South Carolina's attack on a tariff bill. President John Quincy Adams, who was from Massachusetts, had in 1828 signed a law designed to protect the nation's young—and mostly

Northern—manufacturing industry. Southerners, who would have to pay higher prices for manufactured goods, called it the "tariff of abominations." Soon an anonymously published pamphlet, *The South Carolina Exposition and Protest*, promoted the doctrine of nullification. Declaring that the Constitution was no more than a treaty among independent states, the exposition claimed that a state could "nullify" or veto any act of the federal government with which it disagreed. It was discovered that Vice President John Calhoun, a South Carolinian slaveholder, had written the pamphlet, and South Carolina senator Robert Hayne echoed his words on the Senate floor.

Daniel Webster, U.S. senator from Massachusetts. Metal engraving by unidentified artist. *United States Senate Collection.*

Before the Senate and a packed visitors gallery in January 1830, Webster delivered his reply. His towering reputation and the sectional tension created by the tariff act ensured that his speech was highly anticipated. He disagreed with the notion that the United States was simply a confederation of independent states and maintained that it was one, indivisible nation. Webster knew that Southern anxiety over the future of slavery motivated Southerners' arguments for states' rights and nullification, and he addressed the topic directly. He assured them that slavery was not a concern of the central government and explicitly endorsed the policy of noninterference. Webster concluded by criticizing Hayne's (and Calhoun's) claim of "Liberty first and Union afterwards." Webster substituted in its place "that other sentiment, dear to every true American heart, Liberty and Union, now and forever, one and inseparable." A reprint of Webster's speech became a best-selling pamphlet just as Garrison dedicated himself to challenging Webster's confident belief that the Union established a nation dedicated to liberty. The struggle for dominance between the American Revolution's dual legacies of liberty and union would soon bitterly divide Bostonians.

Chapter 2

FIREBRANDS OF LIBERTY

The Liberator's strident attacks on slavery quickly gained the attention of Southern slaveholders. Nat Turner, a slave in Virginia, organized a rebellion involving approximately seventy enslaved and free blacks in August 1831. Before white Virginians succeeded in suppressing the rebellion, Turner and his followers had murdered approximately sixty white men, women and children. Many slaveholders blamed *The Liberator* for inciting Turner despite the absence of evidence that he knew of the newspaper. Of Turner's rebellion, Garrison wrote that while he was horror-struck at the news of violence, "immediate emancipation alone can save [this guilty land] from the vengeance of Heaven, and cancel the debt of ages!"

Garrison seized the moment to seek new converts to the abolitionist cause. In January 1832, he and eleven other radical white abolitionists[4] founded the New England Anti-Slavery Society at a meeting held in the basement schoolroom of the African Baptist Church. The constitution of the society directly attacked racial discrimination and posited that "a mere difference of complexion is no reason why any man should be deprived of any of his natural rights, or subjected to any political disability." The society's purpose was to endeavor "to effect the abolition of slavery in the United States, to improve the character and condition of the free people of color, to inform and correct public opinion in relation to their situation and rights, and obtain for them equal civil and political rights and privileges with the whites." Of the gathering, Garrison presciently predicted, "We have met tonight in this obscure schoolhouse; our numbers are few and our influence limited; but mark my prediction, Faneuil

Boston and the Civil War

The African Meeting House (also known as the First African Baptist Church) on Beacon Hill. This building, which is today part of Boston's Museum of African American History, has been restored to its 1854 appearance. This photo was taken in approximately 1890. *Courtesy of the Massachusetts Historical Society.*

Hall shall ere long echo with the principles we have set forth." The legacy of Faneuil Hall, known as the "cradle of liberty" because prominent Patriots such as Samuel Adams had there urged resistance to British tyranny, would inspire this new generation of activists determined to defy the status quo.

The black community's offering their meetinghouse for this gathering was an important gesture that set a precedent for Boston's interracial cooperation. Members of the Massachusetts General Colored Association also attended the meeting. The following year, the association became an auxiliary of the organization.

The New England Anti-Slavery Society spawned many local antislavery societies, including the integrated Boston Female Anti-Slavery Society, which was established in 1833. Several factors likely explain the rapid sprouting of antislavery societies in and around Boston. The abolitionist movement attracted reformist impulses and evangelical suasion unleashed by the Second Great Awakening. Boston, nicknamed the "city upon a hill" by colonial governor and Puritan John Winthrop, viewed itself as a moral and religious beacon. Great Britain's 1833 abolition of slavery throughout the British Empire demonstrated the potential strength and clout of an abolitionist movement. Critically, the New England Anti-Slavery Society

Maria Weston Chapman.
Courtesy of the Massachusetts Historical Society.

(which changed its name in 1835 to the Massachusetts Anti-Slavery Society) deployed several charismatic antislavery "traveling agents" in a grass-roots strategy that included lectures, antislavery fairs and petition drives. Garrison, who traveled extensively throughout eastern Massachusetts, was likely the most effective agent.

Women were particularly drawn to antislavery work. "As women, as wives, as mothers, we are deeply responsible for the influence we have on the human race," wrote Maria Weston Chapman, a leader of the Boston Female Anti-Slavery Society.[5] She would be a close ally of Garrison's and a leader of Boston's abolitionist movement throughout the antebellum period. By 1837, more than two hundred antislavery societies dotted Massachusetts.

A Mob Attacks Garrison

In 1835, Garrison's followers were still a small minority of Boston's roughly sixty-one thousand whites. However, the abolitionists were increasing in number and visibility. Influential Southerners urged Boston's economic elite to take decisive action against Garrison, and their encouragement fell on receptive ears. An upcoming meeting of the Boston Female Anti-Slavery Society provided an opportunity for conservative Bostonians to demonstrate their opposition to Garrison's inflaming sectional tension. Conservatives viewed the women's society as a particularly inviting target, as they also opposed female activism and were angered by the leadership role assumed by Chapman and other socially prominent women.

The Boston Female Anti-Slavery Society had invited George Thompson, a foremost British abolitionist, to lecture to the society. The first date was postponed amid fears that a mob would disrupt the meeting, as pro-slavery advocates had offered a reward to anyone who laid "violent hands" on Thompson. The meeting was rescheduled for October 21, 1835, although Thompson no longer planned to appear. A false rumor that Thompson would speak circulated shortly before the rescheduled meeting was to begin, and a crowd of several thousand bankers, merchants and others assembled on Washington Street in the heart of downtown Boston. Upon learning that Garrison was present in the lecture hall, the mob focused its attention on him.

To prevent violence, Boston mayor Theodore Lyman and his allies escorted the women attendees to safety. Garrison attempted to escape undetected. Bradley Newcomb Cumings, a twenty-four-year-old clerk in a dry goods store, described the dramatic events in his diary:

> *Garrison escaped by a back window, into a carpenter's shop in Wilson's Lane, where for some time he lay concealed under a heap of shavings, till one of the apprentices gave the information where he was, when he was taken by the crowd into State Street, with the avowed purpose of applying a coat of tar & feathers.*[6]

Garrison was rescued from his captors and a possible lynching only when Mayor Lyman put Garrison in jail overnight to protect him from physical harm. *The Liberator* promptly excoriated the "gentlemen of property and standing" who had perpetrated this riot against free speech in Boston, the "city of Hancock and Adams, the headquarters of refinement, literature, intellect and religion."

The ugliness of the mob and Garrison's close escape brought him fresh notoriety. It also gained him several key allies, most significantly Wendell Phillips, a member of Boston's upper class, and Sarah and Angelina Grimké, daughters of a wealthy slave owner from South Carolina.

WENDELL PHILLIPS

Wendell Phillips was born to a prosperous Boston family. His father, John Phillips, was Boston's mayor from 1822 to 1823, and Wendell attended Harvard College and its law school. Phillips would date his conversion to the abolitionist cause to his outrage when the mob dragged Garrison through Boston's streets. Phillips gave his first public antislavery address in 1837 following the murder of Illinois abolitionist newspaper printer Elijah Lovejoy. Lovejoy's death at the hands of pro-slavery rioters generated national attention as it starkly illustrated the close connection between Southern slavery and the suppression of free speech and civil liberties. Many Bostonians gathered at Faneuil Hall to debate the incident.

The attorney general of Massachusetts was among those who criticized Lovejoy's inflammatory newspaper for fomenting protests. When the attorney general praised Lovejoy's attackers and compared them to the brave men who had dumped British tea into the sea in 1773, Phillips rose to vigorously refute any comparison between Lovejoy's murderers and the Patriot heroes.

Wendell Phillips. *Courtesy of the Library of Congress.*

"The men of the Revolution went for right as secured by law," he declared. "The rioters of today go for their own wills, right or wrong." Phillips went on to cite Boston's special connection to freedom. "When liberty is in danger," he told the crowd, "Faneuil Hall has the right, it is her duty, to strike the keynote for these United States."

Phillips's oratory was so eloquent, passionate and inspiring that he became known as the "golden trumpet" of the abolitionist movement. Phillips's upper-class background also afforded him opportunity to seek converts among Boston's oldest and most influential families. His objections to slavery ran so deep that he reportedly refused to wear cotton because it was produced by the labor of slaves. In the years before the Civil War, Phillips became a leading proponent of disunion, which he favored over a union composed of free and slave states. Soon after his Faneuil Hall speech, Phillips told the Massachusetts Anti-Slavery Society, "Disunion is coming…for the spirit of freedom and the spirit of slavery are contending here for the mastery. They cannot live together."

Sarah and Angelina Grimké

"The Grimké sisters," as they are usually known, were daughters of a wealthy plantation owner in Charleston. Their father also served as chief justice of the South Carolina Supreme Court, and their uncle was the governor of North Carolina. In an extraordinary act of defiance for Southern women, they objected to the immorality and cruelty of slavery and became outspoken abolitionists.

Their conversion began in 1819 when Sarah visited Philadelphia with her dying father, who wished to consult Quaker physicians. Sarah eventually became a member of the Quaker community, and Angelina joined her there in 1828. Witnessing the mistreatment of slaves during visits home to Charleston, coupled with Quaker teachings that condemned slavery, led the sisters to become implacably hostile to the South's "peculiar institution."

In 1835, Angelina wrote a letter to *The Liberator* in which she praised Garrison's passion and positions and said, "It is my deep, solemn, deliberate conviction that this [abolitionism] is a cause worth dying for." The following year, she wrote *Appeal to the Christian Women of the South*, urging Southern women to acknowledge the evils of slavery. Sarah, meanwhile, penned *Epistle to the Clergy of the Southern States*, urging Southern clergy to support the abolitionist cause.

Angelina Grimké. *Courtesy of the Library of Congress.*

Garrison and his allies invited the Grimké sisters to become traveling lecturers for the abolitionist movement. Accompanied by Sarah, Angelina (who was a more confident and polished public speaker) delivered a series of antislavery lectures throughout Massachusetts in 1837 that converted many more to the abolitionist cause. Before the lecture tour began, abolitionist Maria Weston Chapman wrote to all local female antislavery societies urging them to "afford every facility in your power to Sarah M. and Angelina E. Grimké, for the prosecution of their labours in the cause of emancipation."[7] In the five months between June and October, Angelina Grimké lectured nearly eighty times to over forty thousand people and collected over twenty thousand signatures on antislavery petitions.[8] As the sisters came under intense criticism for their public role in opposing slavery, they also became advocates for women's rights. During and after this tour, they published a series of letters that argued for the moral equality of all: black and white, enslaved and free, male and female.

On February 21, 1838, Angelina Grimké became the first woman to address the Massachusetts legislature when she presented the antislavery petitions to state lawmakers. In her remarks, she attacked slavery and defended the rights of women to speak on political issues:

> *I stand before you as a Southerner, exiled from the land of my birth by the sound of the lash and the piteous cry of the slave. I stand before you as a repentant slaveholder. I stand before you as a moral being, and as a moral being I feel that I owe it to the suffering slave and to the deluded master, to my country and to the world to do all that I can to overturn a system of complicated crimes, built up upon the broken hearts and prostrate bodies of my countrymen in chains.*[9]

The sisters gave up public speaking in 1838 following Angelina's marriage to abolitionist Theodore Weld, who opposed injecting the issue of women's rights into the abolitionist movement. But during their brief time in the public spotlight, the Grimké sisters were enormously influential. They gave the young abolitionist movement the authentic voice of members of a slaveholding family able to share personal observations of the institution of slavery. Several years later, the abolitionist movement would gain its most important authentic voice, that of an actual slave—the self-emancipated Frederick Douglass.

Frederick Douglass

Frederick Douglass, born into slavery in Maryland, escaped in 1838 when he was approximately twenty years old. "I have no accurate knowledge of my age, never having seen any authentic record containing it," Douglass later recounted. As a child, his mistress taught him rudimentary reading skills, and when his master ordered his wife to stop, Douglass secretly continued his own education. He later wrote that his master's worry that a literate slave would become dissatisfied planted within him the desire for freedom.

As a young man, Douglass was sent to work for a vicious "slave-breaker" but resisted being beaten. Douglass later credited his resistance with reviving within him the sense of manhood that slavery had nearly extinguished.

Hub of the Second Revolution

When his master subsequently leased him out as a ship caulker in the port of Baltimore, Douglass planned his escape. From a free black seaman he obtained the identification papers that free blacks were required to carry. Anna Murray, a free black woman whom Douglass would later marry, provided him with a sailor's uniform and money for a train ticket. Douglass traveled to Philadelphia and then New York, where Murray joined him. They continued on to New Bedford, Massachusetts, which had both a substantial black community and a thriving shipbuilding industry where Douglass found work.

Within a year of his arrival in New Bedford, Douglass became a subscriber to *The Liberator*. In August 1841, he attended a local antislavery meeting and was moved to share his personal story with the audience. Listeners were captivated by his story and delivery, and abolitionist leaders invited Douglass to a meeting of the Massachusetts Anti-Slavery Society on Nantucket Island. With Garrison's enthusiastic prompting, Douglass soon became an antislavery lecturer. Audiences were riveted as Douglass articulately and passionately described his harrowing experiences as a slave.

In 1845, Douglass wrote his first autobiography, *Narrative of the Life of Frederick Douglass, an American Slave*. This book, which became a bestseller, inspired more Americans to join the growing abolitionist movement. Knowing that many doubted a former slave could write a work of such literary excellence, Garrison and Phillips each wrote prefatory remarks stressing that Douglass was the author of the *Narrative*. Garrison urged readers to

Frederick Douglass soon after publication of his 1845 autobiography. Original image located at the Art Institute of Chicago. *Public domain*.

take action. "What are you prepared to do and dare in their [slaves'] behalf?" he asked. "Be faithful, be vigilant, be untiring in your efforts to break every yoke, and let the oppressed go free…inscribe on the banner which you unfurl to the breeze, as your religious and political motto—'NO COMPROMISE WITH SLAVERY! NO UNION WITH SLAVEHOLDERS!'"

Douglass's decision to publish his autobiography carried serious personal risks. He was a fugitive slave, and the Fugitive Slave Act of 1793 provided for the capture and return of self-emancipated (runaway) slaves. Following the fanfare that attended publication of the *Narrative*, Douglass was in extreme danger from slave hunters. He went abroad to England and Ireland to rally support for the abolitionist cause and returned to the United States two years later—after supporters had purchased his freedom.

The George Latimer Case

Fears of roving slave hunters were very real, even as far north as Boston. In 1842, George Latimer, a self-emancipated slave owned by a Virginia shopkeeper, was captured in Boston. Latimer and his wife had escaped by stowing away on a ship bound for Boston. Unfortunately, a former employee of the shopkeeper recognized Latimer and sent a message to his owner, who demanded Latimer's return. He was arrested and taken to a nearby jail.

Boston's black and white abolitionists immediately mobilized. At a meeting at Faneuil Hall, they resolved that Massachusetts "cannot allow her soil to be polluted by the foot-print of slavery."[10] Sympathetic attorneys pursued redress in court. In 1836, the Boston Female Anti-Slavery Society had brought a case seeking the freedom of a young slave girl, Med, whose master had brought her on a visit to Massachusetts. Lemuel Shaw, the chief justice of the Massachusetts Supreme Judicial Court, had agreed that Med's slave status ended when she set foot on the "free soil" of Massachusetts. In the Latimer case, however, Chief Justice Shaw disagreed with the abolitionists' claim that a "higher" law of freedom trumped Congress's law. He concluded that Congress's fugitive slave law of 1793 governed a case involving a runaway slave and refused to intercede on Latimer's behalf. Unlike Med, Latimer was not in Massachusetts by his master's choice. Shaw's decision confirmed many abolitionists' belief that the U.S. Constitution was a pro-slavery document.

As Latimer remained jailed, many previously indifferent Bostonians became attentive to his future. They did not want to see a man forcibly returned to slavery from Boston, the city where the American Revolution began. Abolitionists created a newspaper, *The Latimer Journal and North Star*, to keep a spotlight on the case. Latimer's status was ultimately settled when his owner agreed to manumit (free) him for $400 after his jailer reported that he could no longer guarantee Latimer's security. Bostonians raised the necessary funds.

Abolitionists were determined to leverage public opposition to Latimer's return to pass a law designed to thwart operation of the fugitive slave law in Massachusetts. As many were eager to keep the taint of slavery off the free soil of Massachusetts, the state legislature enacted a personal liberty law that prohibited any state official from enforcing the fugitive slave law and prohibited state buildings from being used to detain fugitives. By the end of the decade, Southern hostility to Northern defiance over the return of fugitive slaves would help to spark a national crisis.

Collaborating Against Segregated Schools

Interracial cooperation between black and white abolitionists expanded during the late 1840s as they joined forces in a local struggle against segregated schools. This effort both reflected and reinforced the commitment of radical abolitionists to seek civil and political equality while opposing slavery. Black children in Boston were required to attend substandard, segregated schools often located at a considerable distance from their homes. In 1847, black community activist William Cooper Nell collaborated with black lawyer Robert Morris, white lawyer Charles Sumner and black printer Benjamin Roberts to challenge Boston's segregated public school system.

Nell had become an active abolitionist at age fifteen when, peering through a basement window of the African Meeting House, he literally witnessed the birth of the New England Anti-Slavery Society. Nell's father, a leader within the Massachusetts General Colored Association, had helped forge the events of that historic evening. Despite his youth, Nell had already had a scarring encounter with racial prejudice. Two years earlier, while a student at the all-black Abiel Smith School, he was among a small number of Boston students honored for academic excellence. Due to his race, Nell was excluded from a celebratory dinner for award winners. Nell later wrote that his exclusion from that event "deepened into a solemn vow that 'God helping me, I would do my best to hasten the day when the color of the skin would be no barrier to equal school rights.'"

When the New England Anti-Slavery Society was founded, Nell became secretary of the newly established Garrison Independent Society, an organization of youths dedicated to the eradication of slavery and to service to the community. He also served as an apprentice at *The Liberator*, where he learned journalism and sought both subscribers and contributors to the paper. Nell became one of Garrison's closest confidants.

Attorneys Robert Morris and Charles Sumner were also important community leaders. Robert Morris was among the nation's first black lawyers, and he was the first black lawyer in Massachusetts to try a case before a jury. White abolitionist lawyer Ellis Gray Loring had trained Morris after being impressed by his intelligence and diligence while he was working as a household servant. Charles Sumner, a white Harvard-educated lawyer who also lived on the north side of Beacon Hill, would be elected to the U.S. Senate in 1851, where he would strongly condemn slavery and support civil rights

William Cooper Nell. *Courtesy of the Massachusetts Historical Society.*

Robert Morris. *Courtesy of the Social Law Library.*

for blacks. Morris and Sumner brought a legal case, *Roberts v. City of Boston*, challenging Boston's segregated public schools. The plaintiff in the case was printer Benjamin Roberts's five-year-old daughter, Sarah, whose long walk to the all-black Smith School took her past several all-white schools.

Before the Massachusetts Supreme Judicial Court, Sumner argued that segregated schools were inconsistent with the equality before the law that was "declared by our fathers in 1776 and made the fundamental law of Massachusetts." Yet the court rejected the challenge and upheld segregated schools. Although the Massachusetts legislature would order schools integrated in 1855, the legacy of Chief Justice Shaw's 1850 *Roberts* opinion lasted for over a century. He coined the odious doctrine of "separate but equal," which was later adopted by the U.S. Supreme Court and formed a core tenet of this nation's jurisprudence until it was finally rejected in *Brown v. Board of Education* in 1954.

The Liberty and Free Soil Parties

During the 1840s, the abolitionist movement also ventured into the sphere of electoral politics. Garrison and his closest allies (known as "Garrisonians") refused to engage with the political system, as they condemned it as irrevocably contaminated by slavery. But other abolitionists believed in the possibility of change through the power of the vote. In 1840, "political abolitionists" formed a new political party, the Liberty Party, which demanded an immediate end to slavery and claimed that the immoral and "unnatural" fugitive slave clause of the Constitution had no binding force. The Liberty Party fielded James Birney, a repentant former slaveholder from Kentucky, for president in the elections of 1840 and 1844. Birney received far less than 1 percent of the popular vote in 1840 and 2.3 percent in 1844. In Massachusetts, Birney received only 1.3 percent of votes cast in 1840 but—on the heels of the Latimer case—more than 8 percent (over ten thousand) of votes cast in 1844, a total exceeded only by New Hampshire. By 1848, the Liberty Party was largely absorbed into the newly formed Free Soil Party.

The Free Soil movement, which was dedicated to prohibiting the expansion of slavery into new territory, began in response to the nation's 1845 admission of Texas into the Union as a slave state and grew in popularity as a result of the Mexican-American War. When that war ended in 1848, the United States gained an enormous tract of land containing what would become the future states of California, Arizona, Nevada and Utah, as well as portions of Colorado, New Mexico and Wyoming. Suddenly the balance of power previously maintained by the Missouri Compromise of 1820 was threatened. New states meant new senators, and much of the new territory was located below the 36° 30′ parallel. Free Soilers believed in the superiority of a labor system based on "free men engaged in free enterprise on free soil." Many of them also disliked Southern slavery but—for the sake of the Union—were willing to let it continue where it was already established so long as slavery was not extended into new territories.

Although dissatisfied with the limited antislavery demands of Free Soilers, some abolitionists, including many who had formerly supported the Liberty Party, were eager to find political allies. William Nell was among Boston's black activists who supported the Free Soil Party. He was even a Free Soil Party candidate (although unsuccessful) for the Massachusetts state legislature in 1850. The Free Soil Party also drew members from the Whig Party (the so-called conscience Whigs, who were distinguished from the pro-slavery "cotton Whigs") and some members of the Democratic Party. The emergence of the Free Soil Party was the start of a realignment of the nation's political constellation that would include the demise of the Whig Party, the reconfiguration of the Democratic Party into a pro-slavery (and pro-immigrant) party and the birth of the Republican Party.

In 1848, the Free Soil Party held its first national convention and nominated former Democratic president Martin Van Buren for president and Charles Francis Adams of Massachusetts for vice president. Adams was the son of former president John Quincy Adams and the grandson of John Adams. For generations, the Adamses were longtime leading opponents of slavery among Boston's political elite. John Adams had drafted the Massachusetts Constitution that, in effect, outlawed slavery. His wife despised slavery. After serving as president from 1825 to 1829, John Quincy Adams returned to Washington as a congressman. In this role, he became a leading opponent of slavery and led efforts to undermine the "gag rule," a pro-Southern rule intended to bar the presentation of antislavery petitions and debates over slavery. In 1841, in the Amistad case, John Quincy Adams represented Africans who had been illegally kidnapped in violation of laws prohibiting the international slave trade.

Charles Francis Adams was a "conscience Whig" who had served in the Massachusetts House of Representatives and Senate from 1841 to 1846. He established his Free Soil credentials when he opposed the annexation of Texas and the Mexican-American War on the grounds that they would expand slave territory. The 1848 Free Soil Party ran under a banner of "Free Soil, Free Speech, Free Labor, and Free Men." The party platform resolved "no more slave states and no more slave territory" but also emphasized that it intended no interference with slavery in those states where it existed.

The Whigs fielded Zachary Taylor, a military hero of the Mexican-American War. Taylor was also a large slaveholder and owned plantations in Mississippi, Louisiana and Kentucky. Congressman Abraham Lincoln of Illinois was among those campaigning for the Whig Party. Lincoln, who at age thirty-nine was nearing the end of his single term in Congress, visited Massachusetts for ten days in September 1848. He addressed several political gatherings in Boston, including one at the Tremont Temple Baptist Church, the first integrated church in the United States. In words familiar to modern audiences, Lincoln urged followers of the Free Soil Party not to act as third-party spoilers and throw the election to the Democratic Party, which supported letting the settlers in each territory determine whether to allow slavery. Lincoln claimed that the Whig Party agreed with the Free Soil Party on denying the extension of slavery into territories. Lincoln later recalled of his Boston visit, "With hayseed in my hair, I went to Massachusetts, the most cultured State in the Union, to take a few lessons in deportment."

Zachary Taylor won the presidency. Nationally, the Free Soil Party won approximately 10 percent of the popular vote, although it failed to win any electoral votes. In Massachusetts, the Free Soil ticket captured 28.5 percent of the popular vote, a percentage equaled only by Vermont. Taylor died one year into his term as president. His successor, Millard Fillmore, supported Southern demands to extend slavery into the southwestern territories ceded by Mexico. The growing strength of the Northern Free Soil movement coupled with Southern opposition plunged the United States into a crisis. Daniel Webster would be among those determined to craft a new compromise that would neutralize the issue of slavery and protect the future of the Union.

Chapter 3

STARK MAD ABOLITIONISTS

The lines were tensely drawn for the crisis faced by the United States in 1850. Southerners wanted slavery to be allowed in the lands won from Mexico, but the growing number of Free Soil Northerners opposed any expansion of slavery into new territories. Northerners were defying the fugitive slave law by harboring runaway slaves and enacting personal liberty laws designed to shield self-emancipated slaves from recapture. Furious Southerners were determined to punish the North for interfering with their "property." Adding further fuel to the fire, Californians wished to join the Union as a free state, which would upset the delicate equilibrium between free and slave states.

Senator Henry Clay of Kentucky resolved to forge a compromise to this sectional crisis. A leading statesman of his time, Clay had been an architect of the successful Compromise of 1820; he had also served as Speaker of the House of Representatives and secretary of state and had thrice been nominated for president. He believed that a new compromise could, once again, defuse slavery as a divisive, sectional issue.

To settle this new crisis, Clay proposed a multi-part compromise that included the following key provisions: (1) allowing the settlers in new southwestern territories ceded by Mexico to vote on whether to allow slavery ("popular sovereignty"); (2) enacting a new, stringent fugitive slave law; and (3) admitting California as a free state. Abolitionist and Free Soil Bostonians opposed popular sovereignty, as it left the door open for slavery's expansion. They also vehemently opposed the proposed new fugitive slave act that

BOSTON AND THE CIVIL WAR

PRACTICAL ILLUSTRATION OF T

Hub of the Second Revolution

A political cartoon titled "Practical Illustration of the Fugitive Slave Act" depicts the enmity between William Lloyd Garrison and Daniel Webster over the Fugitive Slave Act. In the cartoon, Garrison shields a slave woman while Daniel Webster carries a slave catcher on his back. Garrison and a black man both point guns at the slave catcher. The Temple of Liberty in the background flies two freedom flags. This cartoon is believed to have been created in Boston. *Courtesy of the Library of Congress.*

would, among other harsh provisions, require Northern citizens to cooperate in the seizure of fugitive slaves and appoint special federal commissioners to hear these cases. Disingenuously, Southerners, who claimed to be motivated by "states' rights," were untroubled by the irony that the proposed fugitive slave act would grant the national government broad new powers and strip state courts of the authority to hear a whole class of cases.

Webster's Seventh of March Speech

On March 7, 1850, Daniel Webster took the floor of the U.S. Senate to share his views on the proposed Compromise of 1850. The antislavery community of abolitionists and Free Soilers hoped that Webster, who disliked slavery, would harshly criticize the proposed legislation. But unknown to them, Webster had already indicated to Clay that he would support the proposed compromise. Webster was worried about Southern threats of secession if their pro-slavery demands were not met. He continued to believe that a policy of noninterference with slavery was the best way to ensure the future of the Union he valued above all else.

Webster tipped his hand in his first few words. "I wish to speak today, not as a Massachusetts man, nor as a Northern man, but as an American." Warming to his theme, he urged all Americans to act "for the restoration to the country of that quiet and harmony which make the blessings of this Union so rich and so dear to us all." He declared that sectionalism and threats of secession, not slavery, were the greatest crises facing the nation and called on both sides to accept compromise. Webster criticized Northern opposition to the proposed fugitive slave act as "wrong" and argued that the constitutional provision requiring the return of fugitives was "as binding in honor and conscience as any other article." Webster titled his speech *The Constitution and the Union*, although history remembers it as the "Seventh of March" speech.

Webster's speech was greeted with praise from Southerners and Northern conservatives and derision from his home state's antislavery community. Those Bostonians supporting Webster included wealthy "cotton Whigs" and many working-class men who worried about their employment prospects should sectional strife worsen and endanger cotton supplies to Massachusetts' textile mills.

Abolitionists turned their wrath on Webster. "I know of no deed in American history done by a son of New England to which I can compare this but the [traitorous] act of Benedict Arnold," thundered abolitionist minister Theodore Parker. His words resonated deeply, as his grandfather, Captain John Parker, had led the Minutemen of Lexington into the first battle of the Revolutionary War. Congressman Horace Mann, a member of the Free Soil Party who also pioneered public school reforms, described Webster as "a fallen star! Lucifer descending from heaven."

Ralph Waldo Emerson cuttingly chided, "The word liberty in the mouth of Mr. Webster sounds like the word love in the mouth of a courtesan." Emerson's opinion carried great weight, as he was a celebrated lecturer, a "man of letters" and a leader of Transcendentalism, an intellectual movement centered in Boston that promoted the belief that each individual has the potential to achieve self-realization.

With Webster's support and the brilliant legislative maneuvering of Illinois senator Stephen A. Douglas, Congress enacted each provision of the Compromise of 1850. President Millard Fillmore rewarded Webster—and protected him from the potential wrath of Massachusetts' state legislators (U.S. senators were not elected by popular vote until 1913)—by appointing him secretary of state in July 1850.

Resistance to the Fugitive Slave Act

Boston's black community was especially alarmed by the Fugitive Slave Act of 1850. All self-emancipated slaves were in obvious danger, and free blacks, too, were unsafe. Any black person could potentially be seized, convicted in a federal proceeding that denied the accused the ability to testify or access to a jury and sent to the South as a slave. (In contrast, Mum Bett and Quock Walker [see Chapter 1] had been allowed to testify and have trial by jury in Massachusetts state courts.) The Fugitive Slave Act even offered a financial incentive to the newly appointed federal commissioners to order any accused black person to slavery; a commissioner was paid ten dollars for each alleged fugitive found to be a slave but only five dollars for one declared legally free. Many former slaves in Boston fled to Canada.

Most blacks, however, resolved to remain. Black leaders, including William Cooper Nell and Robert Morris, launched the League of Freedom, which was dedicated to resisting the new law—by arms or any other means necessary. Lewis Hayden, a self-emancipated slave who had arrived in Boston in 1846, served as president of the league. Radical white abolitionists supported the League of Freedom and formed a second organization dedicated to resistance, a Committee of Safety and Vigilance (Vigilance Committee) headed by Reverend Theodore Parker. Its members included Garrison and Phillips. The Vigilance Committee had mostly white members, but several influential blacks, including Lewis Hayden, also joined. The League of Freedom and the Vigilance Committee would collaborate in defying the Fugitive Slave Act.

Lewis Hayden

Lewis Hayden. *Courtesy of the Boston Athenaeum.*

Lewis Hayden would serve as a leader of Boston's black community for decades. Hayden was born into slavery in Lexington, Kentucky, in 1811. He later recalled that his mother had attempted suicide several times—death was her only possible escape from her master's sexual advances and the horrific beatings he administered when she tried to resist. When Hayden's master, a minister, planned to leave Kentucky for Pennsylvania, he sold Hayden and his brothers and sisters at a slave auction. Hayden recalled his helplessness at watching them being sold and his own rage at being swapped for a pair of carriage horses. Hayden later wrote, "It was commonly reported that my master had said in the pulpit that there was no more harm in separating a family of slaves than a litter of pigs."[11]

Hayden learned of the existence of a Northern abolitionist community while traveling through Kentucky with his new master, a peddler, and listening to conversations in inns and taverns. During these years, Hayden married another slave, Esther Harvey, and they had a son. Tragically, his wife and son were both sold to a slaveholder in the Deep South, and Hayden never learned of their fate. "I have one child who is buried in Kentucky, and that grave is pleasant to think of," Hayden later recalled. "I've got another that is sold nobody knows where, and that I can never bear to think of."[12]

Hayden was sold again in 1840 and married Harriet Bell, also a slave, in 1842. Soon thereafter, Hayden and Bell planned their escape. They were assisted by two young white abolitionists, Calvin Fairbank and Delia Webster. Fairbank asked Hayden why he wanted to escape, and Hayden replied, "Because I am a man." The escape involved a treacherous carriage ride to Ohio during which the Haydens sometimes hid, sometimes posed as slaves and sometimes reportedly used flour to lighten the color of their skin. After brief sojourns in Canada and Detroit, the Haydens moved to Boston, lured there by the reputation of the city's abolitionist community.

The Haydens settled on Beacon Hill in 1846 and worshipped at the Twelfth Baptist Church. Hayden served briefly as a lecturer for the Massachusetts Anti-Slavery Society and then established a clothing business that would become one of the most successful black-owned businesses in Boston. Their home on Phillips Street would shelter many self-emancipated slaves in the coming years.

Ellen and William Craft

The League of Freedom and the Vigilance Committee soon had their first opportunity to resist the new Fugitive Slave Act. Southern leaders targeted self-emancipated slaves Ellen and William Craft for capture. The most unlikely of celebrities, the Crafts inspired audiences with the story of their daring escape from slavery in Georgia in December 1848.

While still a slave, dark-skinned William was contracted out by his master to work as a cabinetmaker. Although required to turn over most of his wages to his master, William was able to save a small amount of money. Ellen was a very light-skinned house slave whose life story emblemized the sexual abuse inherent in Southern slavery. A master's rapes had led to the pregnancies of both Ellen's mother and maternal grandmother. Ellen's mistress despised Ellen for her nearly white skin and physical resemblance to her master. As a consequence, Ellen was given by the mistress to her daughter, Ellen's half sister, as a wedding gift. Ellen and William had a "slave marriage," which gave them no legal rights.

The two plotted a uniquely creative and risky escape. Ellen would disguise her race, gender and class and pose as a wealthy white planter's son on a journey north. She would wear men's clothing, tie a bandage around her chin to conceal her smooth skin and place her right arm in a sling to mask her inability to sign her name. William would pose as her slave. Ellen's change of gender was necessary because a white Southern woman would never travel alone with a male slave. The Crafts planned to travel to the free state of Pennsylvania, a journey that would require several rail transfers and a ferry ride. They were both able to obtain several days' leave from their masters at Christmas in 1848, and they hoped this would allow them a substantial head start before their absence was noticed.

The Crafts recounted the details and close calls of their harrowing journey in their autobiographical *Running a Thousand Miles for Freedom*, published in 1860. In Charleston, South Carolina, a railroad official, who was perhaps suspicious of Ellen's appearance, insisted that she sign her name despite her sling-bound arm. Ellen was spared detection when an army officer, who had dined with her en route, offered to sign "Mr. Johnson and slave" on her behalf. In Baltimore, a railroad station attendant refused to sell Ellen tickets when she could not present papers confirming William's

Ellen Craft in the disguise she wore while fleeing from slavery. *Courtesy of the Massachusetts Historical Society.*

status as her slave. They were saved from discovery when people in line behind them, impatient to purchase their own tickets, prevailed upon the attendant to sell the tickets.

Once in Philadelphia, members of the Quaker abolitionist community sheltered the Crafts. Because that city's proximity to the South made it too dangerous for the Crafts to remain there, sympathizers sent the brave couple to Boston, where they were welcomed by the city's abolitionist community. They settled in the Beacon Hill rooming house owned by Lewis and Harriet Hayden. William soon established a furniture-making and repair business and served as vice-president of the League of Freedom, while Ellen worked as a seamstress. The Crafts' lectures about their experiences brought new attention, members and money to the abolitionist cause.

Southern slaveholders, incensed by the Crafts' prominence, were eager to exercise the long arm of the new Fugitive Slave Act in *The Liberator*'s hometown. In October 1850, just weeks after President Fillmore had signed the legislation enacting the Compromise of 1850, two slave catchers from Georgia arrived in Boston. Members of the League of Freedom and the Vigilance Committee pledged to protect the Crafts, by violence if necessary. They harassed the slave catchers whenever they appeared in public. Lewis Hayden vowed to blow up his home with gunpowder if slave catchers or federal marshals attempted to enter. After ten days, the slave catchers left Boston, humiliated and empty-handed.

Despite this victory, the Crafts knew they were not safe and decided to emigrate. They left for Great Britain in 1850 and remained there for twenty years. Before leaving Boston, the Crafts wanted their marriage sanctioned by a clergyman. Reverend Theodore Parker performed the ceremony at the

Theodore Parker. *Courtesy of the Massachusetts Historical Society.*

Lecture of Minister Theodore Parker. This lithograph was published in the *Illustrated London News* on September 27, 1856. *Courtesy of the Library of Congress.*

Haydens' home. Capturing the spirit of Boston's abolitionist community, Parker gave meaningful gifts to the Crafts: a Bible to save their souls and a knife to save their lives.

Shadrach Minkins

Enraged Southern leaders were determined not to let another escaped slave slip through their hands in Boston. The hub's economic elite were eager for an opportunity to demonstrate their fidelity to the Union, its laws and, critically, the control they wielded over Boston. The case of Shadrach Minkins offered another test. Minkins, who had been born into slavery in Virginia in approximately 1814, escaped from the seaport city of Norfolk. He made his way to Boston, where he found employment as a waiter at the downtown Cornhill Coffee House, located a few steps from the courthouse. Minkins had been in Boston for several months when the Fugitive Slave Act became law.

Early in 1851, Minkins's owner, who had learned of the fugitive's whereabouts, sent a slave hunter to Boston armed with an affidavit testifying to Minkins's slave status. Upon receipt of the affidavit, U.S. deputy marshal Patrick Riley prepared an arrest warrant and seized Minkins at the coffeehouse. Observers quickly spread the news, and abolitionist activists gathered inside and outside the nearby courthouse. As Riley and his deputies tried to clear the courtroom and confine Minkins, a group of fifteen to twenty black men rushed in, seized Minkins and fled. The rescuers smuggled Minkins out of Boston, and he made his way safely to Canada. Lewis Hayden was widely believed to be the instigator of the successful rescue. Commenting on the rescue, Theodore Parker found a parallel in Boston's revolutionary past. He exulted, "I think it is the most noble deed done in Boston since the destruction of the tea in 1773."[13]

While abolitionists celebrated, establishment conservatives promised swift recriminations. Daniel Webster denounced the rescue as an act of treason. Conservative newspapers were also outraged. The *Boston Daily Times* fumed, "Boston was disgraced by one of the most lawless and atrocious acts that ever blackened the character of any community…We can regard it as nothing but a complete triumph over law and order, by a band of black ruffians…for whom hanging would be too lenient a punishment.[14]

President Fillmore called for the arrest and prosecution of those involved with the escape. Legal recriminations did follow. Nine members of the black community, including Lewis Hayden and Robert Morris, were charged with violating the Fugitive Slave Act. Several cases, including those against Hayden and Morris, proceeded to trial. Boston jurors voted to acquit Morris, and the case against Hayden was dismissed when the jury could not reach a unanimous verdict. The federal government eventually abandoned the prosecution of the remaining cases.

The rescue of Minkins left frustrated Southerners and Boston's conservatives seething. Abolitionists staunchly declared that nobody would be returned to slavery from Boston. Neither side had long to wait for the next confrontation.

Thomas Sims

On April 3, 1851, less than two months after the arrest of Shadrach Minkins, Bostonians learned of the arrest of Thomas Sims, an escaped slave from

Georgia. Sims, a bricklayer in Savannah, had stowed away on a ship bound for Boston. Sims's owner traced him to Boston and sent a slave catcher to procure a warrant for Sims's arrest. U.S. marshal Charles Devens seized Sims, who spent the night confined in the jury room of the downtown courthouse. These accommodations were necessary because Boston had no federal prison, and the state's personal liberty law prohibited state prisons from housing any person accused of being a fugitive slave.

To prevent sympathizers from rescuing Sims, authorities posted armed guards at the courthouse and encircled it with iron chains. All who entered the courthouse had to bend down to pass beneath the heavy chains. The unintended symbolism was unmistakable. The Southern chain of slavery now encircled a Northern temple of justice.

Abolitionists pursued two strategies, one legal and one nonlegal. This reflected that the Vigilance Committee had among its members both those willing to defy the law and those determined to seek legal redress. Lewis Hayden was among those who devised a daring escape plan. Sims had worshipped at the Twelfth Baptist Church, which was nicknamed the "fugitive slave church" because of the large number of self-emancipated slaves who were congregants. Reverend Leonard Grimes, who as the pastor of the Twelfth Baptist Church was permitted to visit Sims, conveyed a message instructing him to jump out of a courthouse window onto mattresses that abolitionists would place on the street below. But the plan was thwarted when the windows in the room where Sims was held were reinforced with iron bars.

Separately, abolitionist lawyers sought a legal remedy. Seeking to have Sims's case heard by a Massachusetts state court judge rather than a federal commissioner, these lawyers prevailed upon Lemuel Shaw, chief justice of the Massachusetts Supreme Judicial Court, to consider Sims's petition seeking release from unlawful imprisonment. But Shaw determined that the fugitive slave clause of the U.S. Constitution explicitly provided for the return of persons "held to service or labor in one state" and that the new, harsh provisions of the 1850 law did not render it unconstitutional. Shaw's refusal to concede the existence of a higher, moral law prohibiting slavery is believed to have inspired his son-in-law, Herman Melville, to write *Billy Budd, Sailor* and to model Captain Edward Fairfax Vere after Shaw. Captain Vere applies the letter of the law in sentencing seaman Billy Budd to death for the murder of a cruel master at arms despite Budd's moral innocence.

The federal hearing on Sims's status as a fugitive took place before Commissioner George Ticknor Curtis. The lawyer representing Sims's owner

CAUTION!!
COLORED PEOPLE
OF BOSTON, ONE & ALL,

You are hereby respectfully CAUTIONED and advised, to avoid conversing with the

Watchmen and Police Officers of Boston,

For since the recent ORDER OF THE MAYOR & ALDERMEN, they are empowered to act as

KIDNAPPERS
AND
Slave Catchers,

And they have already been actually employed in KIDNAPPING, CATCHING, AND KEEPING SLAVES. Therefore, if you value your LIBERTY, and the *Welfare of the Fugitives* among you, *Shun* them in every possible manner, as so many *HOUNDS* on the track of the most unfortunate of your race.

Keep a Sharp Look Out for KIDNAPPERS, and have TOP EYE open.

APRIL 24, 1851.

A broadside (poster) warning black residents of Boston to be on the lookout for slave catchers and kidnappers. This broadside was created soon after Thomas Sims was returned to slavery in April 1851. *Courtesy of the Library of Congress.*

needed to prove only that the man in custody was the same Thomas Sims identified in the warrant. This was done through the testimony of several witnesses, including crew members of the ship on which Sims had stowed away who testified to discovering Sims just as they entered Boston Harbor. Sims could not testify on his own behalf because the Fugitive Slave Act barred testimony from the alleged fugitive. Commissioner Curtis delivered his opinion on April 11. He found that the accused was the escaped slave Thomas Sims and ordered him returned to slavery.

Daniel Webster supervised the transportation arrangements, which were designed to thwart any possible rescue attempt. At 4:00 a.m., while most of the city slept, police and armed guards escorted Sims to the harbor. Officials placed Sims on board a ship that returned him to Georgia, where his master had him publicly lashed. Angry abolitionists posted new broadsides warning Boston's blacks to "keep a sharp look out for KIDNAPPERS and have TOP EYE open." President Fillmore congratulated Webster on "the triumph of law in Boston," saying, "[S]he has wiped out the stain of the former rescue."[15]

UNCLE TOM'S CABIN AND THE KANSAS-NEBRASKA ACT

Sims was not the last man returned to bondage from Boston. Three years later, in May 1854, the arrest of Anthony Burns gripped both the city and the nation. The political landscape, however, had changed greatly during that time.

Days after Sims's return to slavery, members of the Massachusetts legislature elected Charles Sumner, a member of the Free Soil Party, to the U.S. Senate by a one-vote margin. Sumner, who had served as co-counsel in *Roberts v. City of Boston*, the case that challenged school segregation, vehemently opposed slavery and supported equal rights for blacks. To underscore his disagreement with Webster's policies, Sumner asked, unsuccessfully, for the Senate to repeal the Fugitive Slave Act. Several months later, in October 1852, Daniel Webster died. Boston's conservatives had lost their most eloquent spokesman.

Also in 1852, publication of Harriet Beecher Stowe's *Uncle Tom's Cabin* vividly conveyed the brutalities of slavery to many previously uninterested Northerners. Stowe, who was born to a reformist and deeply religious family, lived in Connecticut until she was twenty-one years old. She then accompanied her father to Cincinnati, Ohio, where he taught at a Protestant seminary. Stowe, who met her husband at the seminary, began writing *Uncle Tom's Cabin* soon after the death of her beloved young son, Charley, in 1849. His death, she said, made her understand "what a poor slave mother may feel when her child is torn away from her."[16] Stowe's primary source for the details of Southern slavery was *American Slavery as It Is: Testimony of a Thousand Witnesses*, written by Sarah Grimké, Angelina Grimké and Angelina's husband, Theodore Dwight Weld, in 1839. This abolitionist tract included numerous firsthand accounts of American slavery by former slaveholders and those who had visited or lived in the South.

Uncle Tom's Cabin was initially published in installments in an antislavery newspaper based in Washington, D.C., and was then published as a book in

Harriet Beecher Stowe, author of *Uncle Tom's Cabin*. *Wilbur H. Siebert Collection, Courtesy of the Ohio Historical Society.*

Boston. The novel contains two storylines, each designed to persuade readers to detest slavery. One story involves the title character, kind and moral Uncle Tom, who is ultimately whipped to death on the order of the demonic overseer Simon Legree. The second story tells of Eliza Harris, a slave mother who escapes north to prevent her baby from being sold away. In a memorable scene, the barefoot Eliza, holding her child, crosses the Ohio River on cracking ice with slave catchers and their bloodthirsty dogs on her heels. Even after reaching a free state, Eliza remains in danger due to the Fugitive Slave Act; she and her husband find safety only after fleeing to Canada.

By using the terror of slavery to drive an engrossing narrative, *Uncle Tom's Cabin* led many Northerners to sympathize with abolitionist efforts. The novel was a runaway bestseller, selling over 300,000 copies in its first year of publication. An oft-told but likely apocryphal story tells of President Lincoln's later meeting with the petite Harriet Beecher Stowe. He reportedly asked her, "Are you the little lady who started this great big war?"

The following year, 1853, saw publication of Solomon Northup's extraordinary slave narrative, *Twelve Years a Slave: Narrative of Solomon Northup, a Citizen of New-York, Kidnapped in Washington City in 1841, and Rescued in 1853, from a Cotton Plantation Near the Red River in Louisiana*. (A feature film based on this book won the 2013 Academy Award for best picture.) This book describes how Northup, who was born free in New York, was kidnapped and sold into slavery and recounts his dozen dreadful years in slavery on a Louisiana plantation. Northup's book served as a continuing reminder that even free blacks were not safe from the possibility of enslavement. While eclipsed in attention by *Uncle Tom's Cabin*, Northup's memoir was reprinted several times, and he dedicated subsequent editions to Stowe.

Also in 1853, the nation's attention had turned to the future territories of Kansas and Nebraska, a portion of the Louisiana Purchase of 1803 that lay north of the 36° 30′ latitude line from which slavery had been permanently banned by the Compromise of 1820. Many Americans were eager to pave the way for new railroad routes and expansion westward, and Illinois Democratic senator Stephen Douglas sought to guarantee a transcontinental route running west from Chicago. To placate Southerners who opposed this northern route, Douglas offered a significant concession—one that would gut the sacrosanct Missouri Compromise. He proposed a deal to bring the railroad north, organize the Kansas and Nebraska territories and allow the future of slavery in Kansas and Nebraska to be decided by the popular vote of their settlers.

Irate, the antislavery community was determined to hold Congress to the terms of the 1820 Compromise. In a passionate speech to the Senate, Charles

Sumner told his colleagues that undoing the Missouri Compromise would be a breach of public faith, an invitation to abolish freedom and a "flagrant and extravagant departure from the original policy of our [founding] fathers." Sumner's sentiments were widely shared in Boston and throughout the state. "In city after city, town after town, newspaper after newspaper, indignant meetings, outraged editorials, and vehement resolutions condemned…[the] 'unholy, treacherous and monstrous proposition.'"[17]

Pro-slavery forces prevailed in Washington, however. Congress passed the Kansas-Nebraska Act in May 1854, and President Franklin Pierce signed it into law. To Boston's antislavery community, the revocation of the Compromise of 1820 epitomized the bad faith of slaveholders and the futility of further compromise. Sumner decried that this act "annuls all past compromises with Slavery, and makes future compromises impossible. Thus it puts Freedom and Slavery face to face, and bids them grapple." It was in this combustible climate that slaveholders again sought to enforce the Fugitive Slave Act in Boston.

Anthony Burns

Anthony Burns was born into slavery in Virginia. His owner, Charles Suttle, frequently contracted out Burns's labor, and prior to his escape, Burns worked loading and unloading cargo on Richmond's wharves. Burns also managed to acquire rudimentary reading and writing skills. In February 1854, he stowed away on a ship bound to Boston. Upon arrival, he found employment at a small clothing store owned by a deacon of the Twelfth Baptist Church. Burns's owner tracked Burns down, and he was arrested as a fugitive on May 24, 1854, the same day that the House of Representatives voted in favor of the Kansas-Nebraska Act. Word of his arrest spread quickly.

Incensed antislavery gatherings took place at several Boston venues. In Faneuil Hall, Wendell Phillips condemned the dual atrocities of that week: "I call [the Kansas-Nebraska Act] knocking a man down, and this [the arrest of Burns] is spitting in his face after he is down." Theodore Parker sarcastically stated that Boston had ceased to exist; it had become a northern suburb of Virginia. He called for an assault on the courthouse the next morning to rescue Burns. Members of Boston's African American community, meeting at nearby Tremont Temple, also called for a rescue attempt. As that meeting ended, some of those leaving Tremont Temple rushed to the courthouse, where they were joined by some of those who had been at Faneuil Hall.

Forcing their way inside, the angry, disorganized mob confronted a marshal and forty to fifty temporary deputies, many of them Irish immigrants, who had been hired to thwart any rescue attempt. Members of the mob used a wooden beam taken from a nearby construction site as a battering ram to breach the doorway into the courtroom where Burns was being held. During the ensuing mêlée, the deputies retained control of their prisoner and successfully pushed back the mob, but one courthouse guard, Irish immigrant James Batchelder, was killed. Several of those involved in the fracas, including Lewis Hayden, were arrested, although their cases were ultimately not prosecuted.

Anthony Burns. *Courtesy of the Library of Congress.*

Abolitionist lawyers Robert Morris and Richard Henry Dana Jr. volunteered to defend Burns in the proceedings before a federal commissioner. Morris and Dana called several witnesses who testified that the man now alleged to be fugitive Anthony Burns had lived and worked in Boston prior to the date on which he was accused of escaping from slavery. The prosecution introduced evidence that the man alleged to be Burns had recognized Suttle when the two men saw each other in the Boston courthouse. While witnesses testified, Reverend Grimes of the Twelfth Baptist Church led efforts to purchase Burns's freedom. He nearly succeeded, but at the last minute, Charles Suttle scuttled the negotiations.

The federal commissioner's decision upheld Suttle's claim and condemned Burns to slavery. Upon learning of the decision, thousands gathered in protest. Several hours later, Bostonians witnessed a horrifying spectacle as nearly two thousand federal troops, local police and hired guards escorted Burns to Boston Harbor to board a boat bound for Virginia. The large number of guards made a last-minute rescue attempt impossible. The walk to the harbor ironically brought Burns alongside Boston's Old State House and the site of the Boston Massacre, revered symbols of the Boston's victory of liberty over tyranny during the American Revolution.

Mary E. Seaver Blanchard, a member of an abolitionist family whose father had recently served as mayor of Boston, described the procession: "In the center of a hollow square formed of volunteers, about 200, all the worst blacklegs and pimps of the city, walked the slave, a good looking fellow. Each one of these men had a drawn sword or knife. Several companies of soldiers marched before and behind, and the Artillery had a six-pound cannon all loaded."[18] Blanchard also described the irate spectators, who greeted the procession with "hisses and shouts," and the funereal look of the city. "Many of the buildings were draped with black," she wrote, "and the Commonwealth building put out a black coffin with the word Liberty upon it."

Upon his return, Suttle punished Burns by chaining him in a small, unsanitary shack for four months. Suttle then sold him to a new owner. However, Reverend Grimes and others had not given up. He was able to purchase Burns's freedom from the new owner for $1,300. Abolitionists paid for Burns to study at Oberlin College. Burns became a minister, but his mistreatment had left him severely weakened, and he died of tuberculosis at age twenty-eight in 1862.

Coming as it did on the heels of both *Uncle Tom's Cabin* and the Kansas-Nebraska Act, the Burns case spurred a revolution in public opinion in Boston. While stalwart conservatives were relieved by Burns's return to slavery, many formerly undecided or even pro-slavery Bostonians were appalled. Blanchard wrote to her father that "almost all are unanimous in feelings of indignation, and mortification, and humiliation." Amos Adams Lawrence, an heir to the Lawrence family whose fortune derived from textile factories, observed, "We went to bed old fashioned conservative Union Whigs and waked up stark mad abolitionists."

The Constitution: Pro-Slavery or Antislavery

On Independence Day 1854, Boston's abolitionists gathered in the suburban town of Framingham to underscore the hypocrisy of the holiday. Garrison wrote in *The Liberator*:

*Raise no starry banner—tears of shame its brightness dims!
On its silken folds, blood-written, see the names of Burns and Sims.*[19]

The crowd heard from many activists and intellectuals, including Wendell Phillips and Henry David Thoreau, whose opposition to slavery had led him to write the seminal essay *Civil Disobedience* in 1849. Advocating a duty to the "higher law," Thoreau observed, "The law will never make men free; it is men who have got to make the law free." When Garrison took his turn at the podium, his passion was literally on fire. Holding a copy of the U.S. Constitution, he proclaimed it a "covenant with death, an agreement with Hell" and burned it before the crowd.

Garrison's dramatic provocation underscored the substantial political divide within the abolitionist movement over whether the U.S. Constitution was a pro-slavery or antislavery document. Garrison and Phillips continued to believe that its compromises with slavery required abolitionists to abstain from political participation. But the growing strength of the Free Soil movement led many to imagine the possibility of success in the political arena. Frederick Douglass and Charles Sumner were among those abolitionists now convinced that the true spirit of the Constitution was freedom and that its endorsements of slavery merely reflected a necessary sectional compromise. As evidence, Douglass and Sumner pointed to other parts of the Constitution, including the Preamble's promise of a more perfect union and the Fifth Amendment's promise that no one could be deprived of life and liberty without due process of law. Most of all, they believed that the promises of life and liberty contained in the Declaration of Independence were embedded within the Constitution. This broader view of the Constitution as a potentially antislavery document would sow the seeds for the antislavery movement's eventual electoral success.

The Rise and Fall of the Know Nothing Party

The Kansas-Nebraska Act and the Anthony Burns case would hasten another realignment of political parties. First, however, came an unfortunate detour that reflected other tensions within Boston. For many voters in Massachusetts, the enormous influx of impoverished Irish Catholic immigrants was an even more pressing issue than slavery. Due in large part to a famine caused by a potato blight, Boston's Irish population exploded during the 1840s and 1850s. In 1830, there were fewer than seven thousand Irish. By 1850, there were thirty-five thousand, and by 1855, nearly fifty thousand Irish-born residents and their offspring crowded the city streets. The Protestant majority objected to the poverty and Catholicism of the Irish immigrants and feared their potential future political power. (See Chapter 7 for a discussion of Boston's Irish community.) The anti-immigrant and anti-Catholic American party erupted onto the scene in 1854 and dominated Massachusetts politics for several years before becoming largely extinct by 1857. The American Party is generally known by its nickname, the Know Nothing Party, which came about because members, many of whom belonged to secret lodges, were instructed to answer questions asked by outsiders by replying, "I know nothing."

In Massachusetts, the Know Nothing Party gained its brief moment of electoral success by espousing both anti-immigrant and antislavery principles. The party overcame the contradictions in those positions through mental gymnastics. "I say [Catholicism and slavery] are in alliance by the necessity of their nature—for one denies the right of a man to his body, and the other the right of a man to his soul," insisted Anson Burlingame, a Boston lawyer elected to Congress as a Know Nothing.[20] The party's candidate, Henry Gardner, was elected governor of Massachusetts in 1854, and the party took control of both houses of the state legislature. Its stunning electoral success was replicated in other Northern states along the eastern seaboard.

The Massachusetts Know Nothing legislature promptly enacted both anti-Catholic and progressive laws. The anti-Catholic laws included requiring public school students to read from the Protestant King James Bible and imposing a two-year residency requirement after naturalization before a new citizen could vote. Progressive legislation included a law requiring the integration of Boston's public schools; this law reversed the decision of Chief Justice Shaw in the case of *Roberts v. City of Boston*. The Know Nothing legislature also strengthened the state's Personal Liberty Law by requiring that a fugitive's status be proved before a state court judge.

The Origin of the Republican Party

During the summer of 1854, the Republican Party, which was formed as an alliance among the Free Soil Party, remaining conscience Whigs and antislavery Democrats, held its first state convention in Michigan. The new name was bestowed by New York newspaper editor Horace Greeley, who wrote the following in a June 1854 editorial:

> *We should not care much whether those thus united* [against slavery] *were designated "Whig," "Free Democrat" or something else; though we think some simple name like "Republican" would more fitly designate those who had united to restore the Union to its true mission of champion and promulgator of Liberty rather than propagandist of slavery.*

Spurred on by reaction to the Kansas-Nebraska Act and the Anthony Burns case, the first convention of the Republican Party of Massachusetts met in Worcester on July 20, 1854, to select a slate of candidates. Influential leaders of Boston's black community supported this new party, and Lewis Hayden and William Cooper Nell were among the unsuccessful candidates who ran on that year's Republican Party ticket for the state legislature.

By 1856, new events, such as "Bloody Kansas" and the caning of Senator Charles Sumner, accelerated the decline of the Know Nothing Party and the growth of the Republican Party. But the legacy of the Know Nothings would linger into the Civil War years. Boston's Irish immigrants would eschew the Republican Party and loyally back the pro-immigrant and anti-abolitionist Democratic Party.

Chapter 4

THE LEXINGTON OF 1861

Bloody Kansas. The caning of Charles Sumner. Dred Scott. Harpers Ferry. All of these pivotal events had a strong connection to Boston. As they reinforced the South's opposition to any compromise that would limit slavery's expansion, they led more Northerners to join the Republican Party. Together, these events created a rising tide that culminated in the ascension of Abraham Lincoln to the presidency, the secession of South Carolina from the Union, the formation of the Confederacy and the start of a long and bloody civil war. Soldiers from Massachusetts would become the first to die in combat in an incident christened "the Lexington of 1861." The memory of their Patriot ancestors who had fought for the nation's independence would spur Bostonians of all political persuasions, conservatives and abolitionists alike, to rally in support of the Union.

BLOODY KANSAS AND THE CANING OF CHARLES SUMNER

The Kansas-Nebraska Act of 1854, which provided for the votes of settlers in those territories to decide the future of slavery ("popular sovereignty"), led directly to Bloody Kansas, a series of violent confrontations between pro- and antislavery settlers. Nebraska is located sufficiently far north that its future as a free state was assured, but Kansas, which lies immediately west of Missouri, became a battleground. Slaveholders were determined to obtain two more pro-slavery senators, demonstrate that slavery was a thriving labor system and prevent runaway slaves from seeking sanctuary in Kansas. Abolitionist and Free Soil Northerners were equally resolute that the footprint of slavery not be extended. Eager to obtain a majority of eligible voters, pro-slavery Southerners and antislavery Northerners both sent settlers to the Kansas territory. These groups of settlers harassed and sometimes terrorized each other in a series of attacks known as "Bloody Kansas."

These events led directly to a vicious assault on Massachusetts senator Charles Sumner. On May 19 and 20, 1856, he delivered a five-hour speech on the floor of the United States Senate in which he bitterly criticized the "slave powers" for their "rape of a virgin territory" due to the "depraved desire for a new slave state, hideous offspring of such a crime." Continuing with his sexually explicit metaphor, Sumner singled out for special condemnation South Carolina senator Andrew Butler, a key author of the Kansas-Nebraska Act. "The senator from South Carolina," said Sumner, "has chosen a mistress to whom he has made his vows, and who, though ugly to others, is always lovely to him…I mean the harlot, slavery." Sumner further accused Butler of making arguments "with incoherent phrases [that] discharge the loose expectorations of his speech." Butler had recently suffered a disabling stroke, and Sumner's remarks seemed pointedly to mock Butler's condition.

Preston Brooks, Butler's cousin and a congressman from South Carolina, was determined to avenge Butler's honor. Brooks considered challenging Sumner to a duel but abandoned that idea on the grounds that Sumner was not worthy of such a "gentlemanly" challenge. While Brooks planned his revenge, Kansas became

Charles Sumner, U.S. senator from Massachusetts. *Courtesy of the Boston Public Library.*

Hub of the Second Revolution

Detail of an engraving by J.L. Magee showing Representative Preston Brooks caning Senator Charles Sumner. *Courtesy of the Library of Congress.*

bloodier. On May 21, the day after Sumner's speech, a mob of nearly eight hundred slavery supporters sacked and looted the town of Lawrence, Kansas, a town founded by antislavery settlers from the New England Emigrant Aid Society and named after its benefactor, Bostonian Amos Adams Lawrence.

Sumner spent the afternoon of the following day, May 22, in the deserted Senate chamber. Sitting at his desk, which was bolted to the floor, Sumner was signing copies of his "Crime Against Kansas" speech for distribution to supporters. Approaching Sumner from behind, Brooks used his gold-headed cane to viciously beat Sumner over the head. In a desperate attempt to escape, Sumner wrenched his desk loose, but Brook's blows continued to rain down on the defenseless senator until he was rendered unconscious and covered in blood. The beating ceased only when Brooks's cane broke.

The diverse reactions to the caning of Sumner revealed the gulf between the North and the South. Southerners found Sumner's punishment deserved and sent Brooks dozens of new canes, many inscribed with messages of congratulations. The Southern press, too, praised Brooks's violent act. The *Richmond Enquirer*, for example, wrote that abolitionists "must be lashed into submission" and recommended that Sumner "in particular, ought to have nine-and-thirty early every morning. He is a great strapping fellow, and could stand the cowhide beautifully."

Most Bostonians were irate. To them, the savage attack—and the South's conferring celebrity status on Brooks—confirmed the brutality of a slave society that operated without moral or legal constraints. "I do not see how a barbarous community and a civilized community can constitute one state," observed Ralph Waldo Emerson. Even those Bostonians minimally concerned with the expansion of slavery were distressed by the vicious beating within the walls of the Capitol.

Sumner's head injuries were so severe that he remained absent from the Senate for two and a half years. His vacant seat served as a poignant reminder of the violence inherent in a slave society. When Sumner finally returned in 1860, his hatred of slavery was undiminished. He titled his first speech following his return "The Barbarism of Slavery."

The Election of 1856

The caning of Charles Sumner accelerated the demise of the short-lived Know Nothing Party and the rise of the Republican Party. In June 1856, the Republican Party nominated its first presidential candidate, John C. Fremont, a military hero of the Mexican-American War and famed explorer of the American West. The Republican platform proclaimed slavery a "relic of barbarism" and announced that the principles of the Declaration of Independence prohibited slavery's expansion into any territories.

During the months leading up to the election, the Republican Party campaigned against Bleeding Kansas and Bleeding Sumner and for "free soil, free labor, free speech, free man, and Fremont." In a reflection of the swiftly growing appeal of the Republican Party, Fremont won eleven of the sixteen free states, although Democrat James Buchanan won the presidency. In Massachusetts, Fremont won nearly 64 percent of the popular vote. Meanwhile, 23 percent of Massachusetts voters supported Buchanan, and 11.5 percent supported former president Millard Fillmore, who ran as the candidate of both the Know Nothing and Whig Parties.

Garrison reacted to the election of 1856 with mixed emotions. Fremont's electoral strength and the Republican Party's harsh criticisms of slavery demonstrated the enormous successes of the abolitionist movement over a quarter century. But Buchanan's victory confirmed continuing Southern control over the federal government. Even as increasing numbers of abolitionists enthusiastically backed the Republican Party,

Garrison continued to believe that the Constitution sanctioned a union with slavery.

Garrison and Wendell Phillips were key participants at a Disunion Convention organized by radical abolitionist and minister Thomas Wentworth Higginson and held in Worcester, Massachusetts, in January 1857. The convention asserted that the Union was a "hopeless attempt to unite under one government two antagonistic systems of society," supported a separation between the free and slave states and pledged to urge all opponents of slavery to consider the "practicability, probability, and expediency" of disunion. Not surprisingly, conservative Northerners deplored disunion. They saw little difference between Northern supporters of disunion and Southern supporters of secession. Both threatened the Union.

THE DRED SCOTT CASE

The Supreme Court's 7–2 decision in *Dred Scott v. Sanford* in March 1857 held that Congress lacked the authority to restrict slavery in any territories acquired after the creation of the United States. Because this decision annulled the Republican Party's ability to promise to limit slavery to the states where it existed, Southerners hoped that the party would wither and die. But the opposite occurred. The *Dred Scott* case bolstered the Republican Party and brought the nation one large step closer to war.

The facts underlying the momentous case were straightforward. An army surgeon had brought his slave, Dred Scott, from Missouri to live on military bases in the free state of Illinois and the free territory of Wisconsin. After Scott was brought back to Missouri, he sued for his freedom. He argued that his residency on free soil had ended his slave status. Massachusetts had endorsed that view twenty years earlier in the case of the slave child Med.

However, the Supreme Court ruled against Scott. Chief Justice Roger G. Taney's far-reaching opinion announced that no person of African descent—whether free or slave—could ever be a citizen of the United States, thereby revoking the citizenship of free blacks throughout the nation. Taney also decreed that the Constitution denied Congress the authority to ban slavery from any territory, by popular sovereignty or any other means. This sweeping opinion invalidated the Missouri Compromise of 1820 as well as the Kansas-Nebraska Act. Indeed, the logic of the opinion implied that slavery might be allowed anywhere a slave owner traveled and that "some future decision of the pro-slavery majority of the Supreme Court will authorize a slave driver…to call the roll of his manacled gang at the foot of the monument on Bunker Hill."[21]

Supreme Court justice Benjamin Robbins Curtis of Massachusetts penned a furious dissent. Curtis asserted that the framers of the Constitution had hoped that slavery would be gradually abolished and that expanding its footprint ran contrary to their intention. Moreover, as five of the original thirteen states had allowed blacks to be citizens when the Constitution was adopted, he reasoned that no basis existed for the court's conclusion that only whites could be citizens.

Curtis's dissent illustrates the transformation that had occurred among many formerly conservative Bostonians. Curtis had, in 1836, defended Med's owner when the slave child sued for her freedom. In 1850, Curtis had defended the Compromise of 1850, including the Fugitive Slave Act, and Senator Daniel Webster had championed Curtis's nomination to the Supreme Court the following year. In a clear indication of changing times, Curtis resigned from the Supreme Court six months after the *Dred Scott* case was decided.

Outrage at the court's opinion reverberated throughout Boston. Abolitionists distributed copies of Curtis's dissent in pamphlet form and denounced Taney's opinion. More Bostonians joined the Republican Party. Former congressman Abraham Lincoln of Illinois was among those who harshly criticized the court's ruling. Lincoln also maintained that the court's opinion was so at odds with the nation's history and so tainted by "partisan bias" that it should not be treated as establishing settled doctrine for the nation.

In November 1857, eight months after the *Dred Scott* decision, a new cultural and literary magazine, the *Atlantic Monthly*, debuted in the Hub. Many of the city's leading intellectuals were among its founders, including Henry Wadsworth Longfellow, Ralph Waldo Emerson and Oliver Wendell Holmes Sr. James Russell Lowell, a committed abolitionist, was the magazine's editor. The second issue of the *Atlantic Monthly* contained a blistering attack on slavery written by Edmund Quincy, an abolitionist and member of one of Boston's most prominent families; his father had served as mayor of Boston and president of Harvard University. Quincy's essay, "Where Will It End?" compared the North and South and claimed that slavery was the cause of the South's economic, moral and cultural backwardness. Urging Northerners to take a decisive stand against slavery's territorial and political encroachment, Quincy wrote, "True prosperity can never grow up from wrong and wickedness…But that the stronger [Northern] half of the nation should suffer the weaker to rule over it…is indeed a marvel and a mystery." The intellectuals who wrote for the *Atlantic Monthly* would be hugely influential in shaping Northern public opinion in Boston and beyond.

Crispus Attucks Day

Boston's black community was outraged by the *Dred Scott* opinion. Besides sanctioning slavery, the court's opinion had annulled the citizenship of free blacks. Community leaders reacted by denouncing the decision and publicly celebrating the important contributions of black citizens throughout American history. William Nell and John Rock together organized Boston's first Crispus Attucks Day in March 1858 to commemorate the black man who was among the five slain by the British during the Boston Massacre of March 5, 1770.

By this time, Nell had become the first published black historian in the nation. In 1851, he had published a pamphlet, *Service of the Colored American in the Wars of 1776 and 1812*, which he revised into a book titled *The Colored Patriots of the American Revolution*. Nell's works reviewed the key roles that black Americans had played in the nation's founding and wars and thoroughly refuted Chief Justice Taney's claims that the United States was founded by and for whites only. Nell also wrote with another goal in mind. Illustrating the past military service of black Americans would, he believed, help to convince the federal government that blacks should participate in a war against slavery, should one come.

John Rock, who had arrived in Boston in 1853, had rapidly emerged as a leader within Boston's black community. Born in 1825 in New Jersey to free Northern blacks, Rock had sought to obtain a professional education. When his race precluded his admission to medical school, he studied dentistry. Ultimately, Rock was able to attend the American Medical College in Philadelphia and open a medical practice there. He moved to Boston the following year, as he believed that it offered a better racial climate. In Boston, Rock practiced both medicine and dentistry; as a member of the Twelfth Baptist Church led by Reverend Louis Grimes, Rock frequently treated self-emancipated blacks. By 1855, he had a reputation as an effective leader and public speaker. When his health declined during the next several years, Rock would turn to the less physically demanding study of law and earn admission to the Massachusetts Bar. At the 1858 Crispus Attucks Day

John Rock. This portrait was published in *Harper's Weekly* on February 25, 1865. *Courtesy of the Library of Congress.*

celebration at Faneuil Hall, Rock forecast impending violence and the resulting need for blacks to provide military service: "Sooner or later, the clashing of arms will be heard in this country, and the black man's services will be needed."

John Brown and Harpers Ferry

John Brown's daring raid on the federal armory in Harpers Ferry, Virginia, in October 1859 is often described as the spark that ignited the Civil War. In the South, calls for secession grew louder. In the North, this event and its aftermath precipitated the further ascendency of the Republican Party and the election of Abraham Lincoln to the presidency.

Brown, a white man, had pledged his life to the destruction of slavery following the 1837 murder of abolitionist newspaper publisher Elijah Lovejoy in Illinois. Brown scorned talk and moral suasion and favored direct, violent action. After passage of the Kansas-Nebraska Act, Brown brought his antislavery militancy to Kansas. In 1856, in retaliation for the raid on Lawrence, Kansas, carried out by slavery supporters, Brown led a small band that killed five pro-slavery settlers in an event known as the Pottawatomie Massacre.

Soon thereafter, Brown set his sights on an assault that would strike into the very heart of the South. He planned an attack on the Harpers Ferry Armory. His goal was to arm local slaves with weapons stolen from the federal armory and foment an armed rebellion. To raise the money, men and supplies necessary for this daring assault, Brown turned to Boston.

Six men, who would later become known as the "Secret Six," offered Brown financial aid. Five of them lived in or near Boston. They were ministers Theodore Parker and Thomas Wentworth Higginson; physician Samuel Gridley Howe, whose wife would write "Battle Hymn of the Republic"; Boston industrialist George Luther Stearns; and Concord resident Franklin Sanborn. Several of Boston's black leaders, including Lewis Hayden and John Rock, are believed to have also helped raise funds and assemble recruits.[22]

Ultimately, five black and sixteen white men joined Brown at Harpers Ferry. The raid began on October 16, 1859, when Brown led eighteen men (three remained behind as a rear guard) in the attack. At first, events unfolded as Brown had intended—his raiders captured the armory and took hostages from nearby farms. But Brown and his men soon came under attack, initially by the local community and then by U.S. Marines commanded by Colonel Robert E. Lee. Several of Brown's raiders managed to escape, and the rest, including Brown, took refuge in the engine house, a small building at the entrance to the armory. The marines broke down the engine house door and took Brown and seven surviving raiders into custody. The other raiders were killed.

Boston's conservatives immediately condemned Brown's violence and lawlessness. The anti-Republican *Boston Courier* newspaper appealed to those conservatives who had joined the Republican Party "to turn aside at once from leaders, whose political doctrines conduct to disorder, plunder and murder." Many moderate antislavery Bostonians criticized Brown's violent means and his attacking slavery not in a disputed territory but in a state where the Republican Party had pledged noninterference. Initially, even Garrison, who was still devoted to nonviolence, called the raid "misguided." Frederick Douglass stated, however, that Brown's actions "imitated the heroes of Lexington, Concord, and Bunker Hill."[23] (Although Douglass had by then moved to Rochester, New York, he was a frequent visitor to Boston.)

Brown was charged with murder, treason and conspiracy to foment a slave rebellion and placed on trial. He defended his actions as "righteous" and said, "Now, if it is necessary that I should forfeit my life, for the furtherance of the ends of justice, and mingle my blood further with the blood of my children, and with the blood of millions in this slave country, whose rights are disregarded by wicked, cruel and unjust enactments, I say, let it be done." A Virginia jury convicted him, and he was sentenced to death.

By the time Brown was hanged six weeks later, his clearly articulated willingness to die for the abolitionist cause had led many abolitionists to compare him to a Christian martyr. The influential Ralph Waldo Emerson swayed public opinion when he declared that Brown made "the gallows as glorious as the cross." Henry David Thoreau defended Brown's commitment to a "higher law" and pronounced him a "crucified hero." Garrison also rethought his earlier criticism of Brown, stating:

> *Was John Brown justified in his attempt? Yes, if Washington was in his; if Warren* [hero of the Battle of Bunker Hill] *and Hancock were in theirs. If men are justified in striking a blow for freedom when the question is one of a three penny tax on tea, then, I say, they are a thousand times more justified, when it is to save fathers, mothers, wives and children from the slave coffle and the auction block.*[24]

John Rock, speaking at the next Crispus Attucks Day, declared his belief in insurrections of both the "pen and the sword." He observed that "the only events in this history of this country which I think deserve to be commemorated are the organization of the Anti-Slavery Society and the insurrections of Nat Turner and John Brown."

To Southerners, Brown was a terrorist, and his actions, coupled with the support and sympathy he received from some in the North, increased Southern calls for secession. The *Richmond Enquirer* wrote that the Harpers Ferry raid "revived, with ten-fold strength, the desire of a Southern confederacy." The *Charleston Mercury* stated definitively, "The time has arrived in our history for a separation from the North." As 1860 dawned, the North and the South were on a collision course.

Hub of the Second Revolution

The Election of 1860

The four candidates running in the presidential election of 1860 reflected the stark sectional divisions within the nation. Backed by the *Dred Scott* decision, many Southerners argued that no government, federal or local, could restrict slavery in the territories. Southern rejection of "popular sovereignty" led the Democratic Party to split into Northern and Southern wings, hold rival conventions and nominate two candidates for the presidency. Northern Democrats nominated Stephen A. Douglas of Illinois, who continued to support the doctrine of popular sovereignty, while Southern Democrats nominated John C. Breckinridge of Kentucky.

The Republicans were expected to nominate Senator William Seward of New York, an ally of the more radical wing of the party, but the convention instead nominated the more moderate Abraham Lincoln. As in 1856, the Republican Party platform pledged to leave slavery alone in the Southern states but opposed its expansion to any new territories or states, since "the normal condition of all the territory in the United States is that of freedom." The Republican Party platform also denounced all schemes for disunion, whether from Southern conservatives or Northern abolitionists.

Boston's abolitionist community generally supported Lincoln and believed his election would advance the broader antislavery cause. The more the Republican Party expressed hostility to the institution of slavery, the smaller the philosophical gap between the abolitionists and the Free Soilers became. Ultimately, abolitionists hoped, the logic and language of freedom—coupled with Southern intransigence—would compel the Republican Party to embrace total emancipation.

Abolitionist and future governor John Albion Andrew

Abraham Lincoln as a presidential candidate in 1860. *Courtesy of the Library of Congress.*

was among Lincoln's most enthusiastic supporters in Boston. Andrew had been elected to the state legislature in 1856. After serving only one term, he had returned to his private law practice but remained politically active. Following John Brown's raid at Harpers Ferry, Andrew offered to help finance legal counsel for Brown and sought donations to assist Brown's family. Attempting to walk a fine line between praising Brown's intentions but not his acts, Andrew said, "I pause not now to consider…whether the enterprise of John Brown and his associates in Virginia was wise or foolish, right or wrong; I only know that whether the enterprise itself was one or the other, John Brown himself is right." Andrew's nomination for governor at the state Republican convention was a triumph for the abolitionists. Sumner, attending for the first time since his beating, made a moving plea for Andrew's nomination.

In May 1860, Andrew attended the Republican national convention in Chicago. Although Andrew went as a supporter of William H. Seward, who was favored over Lincoln by most abolitionists, he returned home a strong admirer of Lincoln. "I would trust my country's cause in the care of Abraham Lincoln as its chief magistrate, while the wind blows and the water runs."[25]

The fourth party vying for the presidency, the Constitutional Union Party, was composed of voters who were eager to avoid any talk of disunion or secession. Seeking to reassure Northern and Southern Unionists, Constitutional Unionists took no official position on slavery and pledged themselves only to the supremacy of the Union. Party nominee John Bell, a Tennessee slaveholder, ran on a ticket with Edward Everett of Massachusetts. Everett, an heir to Daniel Webster's view of the sacredness of the Union, had formerly served as Harvard president, Massachusetts governor and U.S representative, senator and secretary of state. His supporters included former

Massachusetts governor John Albion Andrew. *Used with permission of istock.com.*

"cotton Whigs" who feared the economic disruptions of war and especially the loss of Southern cotton.

The election was really two elections, since different candidates appeared on ballots in the North and the South. In the North, the race was primarily between Lincoln and Douglas with a small minority supporting Bell. In the South, the race was between Breckinridge and Bell; Lincoln did not even appear on the ballot in most of the Southern states. The *Atlantic Monthly* endorsed Lincoln. Editor James Russell Lowell wrote, "We believe that this election is a turning-point in our history; for, although there are four candidates, there are really, as everybody knows, but two parties and a single question that divides them."

Lincoln won the presidency, and Andrew was elected governor of Massachusetts. Lincoln carried seventeen free states, including Massachusetts, where nearly 63 percent of voters supported Lincoln. Bell garnered just over 13 percent of the states' votes, and Douglas won 20 percent.

The Massachusetts antislavery community was elated by the election results. Just several months earlier, Wendell Phillips had criticized Lincoln's moderate positions and denounced him as the "slave-hound of Illinois." But Phillips now hyperbolically proclaimed, "The slave has chosen a President of the United States." Likely, Phillips's change of heart was not caused by anything that Lincoln had done but rather by "how Americans had rallied around Lincoln with an outpouring of antislavery feeling."[26]

Secession

In the South, Lincoln's election was greeted with threats of secession. Many Northerners initially regarded these as simply the South's again "crying wolf," as reactionary Southerners had called repeatedly for secession in past years. But this time was different. For decades, presidents had supported Southern slave interests. Now the South had lost an election, and it refused to be bound by the verdict. As secession, war and attendant economic disruption became more likely, some of Boston's conservatives lashed out at radical abolitionists, whom they blamed for inciting war. One such altercation took place on December 3, 1860, when black and white abolitionists gathered at Tremont Temple to mark the first anniversary of the hanging of John Brown. A disruptive mob came determined to shut down the meeting. They succeeded, in a scene that was reminiscent of the long-ago day in 1835 when Garrison was nearly lynched in Boston's streets. But this was practically a last gasp for those Bostonians who still sought compromise with the South.

On December 20, a secession convention meeting in Charleston, South Carolina, unanimously voted to adopt the Declaration of the Immediate Causes Which Induce and Justify the Secession of South Carolina from the Federal Union. These causes included "encroaching on the reserved rights of the states," "denouncing as sinful the institution of slavery," assisting slaves to escape, inducing "servile insurrection" and "the election of a man to the high office of President of the United States, whose opinions and purposes are hostile to slavery." By the end of January, five other states had followed South Carolina's lead, and five additional states would follow. The seceded states formed the Confederate States of America and selected Jefferson Davis as president and Alexander Hamilton Stephens as vice president. The cornerstone of the Confederacy "rests upon the great truth that the negro is not equal to the white man; that slavery, subordination to the superior race, is his natural and normal condition," announced Stephens.

In response to secession, Bostonians of all political persuasions temporarily shelved their disagreements over slavery and vowed to preserve the Union. At his inauguration on January 5, 1861, Governor Andrew, despite his abolitionist sympathies, sidestepped the issue of slavery, stating that "there is but one issue before the country now...the federal union must be preserved." Referring to the state's heroism during the American Revolution, he declared that Massachusetts "is willing to make the same sacrifices again, if need be, in the same cause."[27] Among Andrew's first official acts was ordering a one-hundred-gun salute on the Boston Common in honor of past and present patriots.

Andrew began to prepare Massachusetts for war. He ordered a review of the rolls of all state militia companies. The commanding officer of each company was to ascertain whether any men in the unit would be, because of "age, physical defect, business or family causes," unable to respond to a request from the president for troops and, if so, to discharge those men and fill the places with men "ready for any public exigency which may arise."[28] Thanks to Andrew's advance planning, Massachusetts' regiments would be the first to respond to Lincoln's call for troops when war began.

Hub of the Second Revolution

Fort Sumter

Lincoln was inaugurated as the nation's sixteenth president on March 4, 1861. In his inaugural address, he emphasized that the Union was perpetual and indivisible and promised that any use of arms against the United States would be viewed as rebellion and met with force. He also reassured Southerners that he had no intention of interfering with slavery in those states where it existed.

Lincoln also promised to "hold, occupy, and possess" the lawful property of the United States government. This was a reference to Fort Sumter, located in the harbor of Charleston, where eighty-five U.S. troops were stationed. In the months between Lincoln's election and his inauguration, the newly seceded states had seized numerous Federal forts and arsenals within their borders and claimed them as the property of the Confederacy. Fort Sumter remained under Federal control. When Lincoln announced that he would resupply the troops with necessary provisions, the Confederates issued an ultimatum to Fort Sumter commander Robert Anderson: surrender immediately or be fired upon. He refused to surrender. Early the next morning, April 12, 1861, the Confederates opened fire. Following thirty-four hours of a relentless bombardment—which, astonishingly, led to no fatalities—Anderson surrendered. News of the Confederacy's attack and Fort Sumter's surrender shocked, angered and united Boston. Within days, even more inflammatory news would arrive: a secessionist mob would fatally injure four Massachusetts soldiers.

The Lexington of 1861

When Fort Sumter surrendered, Lincoln asked the Union states to send seventy-five thousand volunteers for ninety days' service to defend the nation's capital, "repossess the forts, places, and property which have been seized from the Union" and suppress the rebellion. Already prepared, Massachusetts responded with four regiments of volunteer militia. The men of the Sixth Massachusetts Volunteer Militia, who mostly hailed from the textile cities of Lawrence and Lowell, arrived in Boston on April 16 and were quartered overnight in Faneuil Hall. One soldier wrote home, "The old cradle of liberty rocked to its foundation from the shouting patriotism of the gallant sixth…The city is completely

Boston and the Civil War

The Lexington of 1861. This Currier & Ives lithograph shows Massachusetts troops and secessionists battling in the streets of Baltimore shortly after the fall of Fort Sumter. This event had important symbolic significance to Bostonians. The first Massachusetts men to die in combat during the Civil War fell on the anniversary of the battles of Lexington and Concord, the day in 1775 when "the shot heard 'round the world" signified a new birth of freedom. *Courtesy of the Library of Congress.*

filled with enthusiasm; gray-haired old men, young boys, old women and young, are alike wild with patriotism."[29]

On April 17, the Sixth Massachusetts Volunteer Militia left by train for Washington. The trip would require the troops to change trains—and train stations—in Baltimore. Horse-drawn railcars would transport the troops from one station to the other across the city, where they would board a train line with service to Washington, D.C.

The militia's commanders knew the exposed route through Baltimore's streets might be perilous. Maryland was a "border state," a slave state that had not left the Union to join the Confederacy (the other border states were Delaware, Kentucky and Missouri). The designation of border state might seem to imply neutrality, but in fact, the people of Maryland had intense but divided sympathies. Baltimore itself had a large number of abolitionists and the nation's largest population of free blacks, but many in the city were zealously committed to the perpetuation of slavery.

The militiamen arrived in Baltimore on the morning of April 19, the eighty-sixth anniversary of the Revolutionary War battles of Lexington and

Concord, where Massachusetts men had fired "the shot heard 'round the world." As the men of the Sixth Volunteer Militia journeyed across the city, a mob of Baltimore secessionists blocked several rail cars from passing. When the troops disembarked to continue on foot, members of the mob assaulted them with stones and bricks. Eventually, some members of the mob shot at the troops. During the ensuing mêlée, some soldiers fired into the crowd. By the time a semblance of order was restored, four Massachusetts soldiers and twelve civilians were dead and over one hundred people were wounded.

Back home in Massachusetts, people were quick to connect the events of April 19, 1775, and April 19, 1861. In both cases, sons of Massachusetts had perished at the hands of those bent on destroying the nation, and April 19 was now "rendered doubly sacred." Bostonians of all political stripes found common ground. Edward Everett of the Constitutional Union Party announced, "We forget that we ever had been partisans; we remember only that we are Americans and that our country is in peril." Amos A. Lawrence wrote, "Every man wishes to be a volunteer. Business is suspended, political asperities have ceased and we all stand as one man for the Government." Governor Andrew sought to take advantage of this newfound unity, casting the war as "the struggle of the People to vindicate their own rights, to retain and invigorate the institutions of their fathers." He added, "therefore while I do not forget, I will not name today that 'subtle poison' which has lurked always in our national system."[30]

Abolitionists, too, stood with the Union. Sumner wrote, "I never believed that the North would be practically divided when the conflict came; but I did not expect the ferocious unity and high-strung determination which are now witnessed." Even Garrison and Phillips now became staunch unionists. Phillips, who had called for disunion just days before the Fort Sumter fell, now merged his call for emancipation with a call for union and even admitted having mistaken the extent to which Massachusetts was "wholly choked with cotton dust and cankered with gold."

Garrison's and Phillips's abandonment of their prior commitment to disunion may seem paradoxical, given Lincoln's pledge not to interfere with slavery where it existed. But Garrison was convinced that the North was "rushing like a tornado in the right direction"[31] and that abolitionists would, with meticulous planning and persistent pressure, be able to control the direction of the wind. As war began, Boston's abolitionists therefore adopted a multi-prong strategy. They would support Union war efforts while ceaselessly working to convince Lincoln and Free Soil Republicans that the moral and political survival of the Union required the extinction of slavery.

Five soldiers in Union uniforms of the Sixth Regiment Massachusetts Volunteer Militia. Four are unidentified; Albert L. Burgess appears on the far right. *Courtesy of the Library of Congress.*

Joined by free blacks, they would argue that military and moral victory required the participation of black soldiers.

In arguing for total emancipation, the abolitionists' greatest strategic allies would be Southern military prowess and Southern political intransigence. Southern military victories would ensure that the war would last long enough for the abolitionists to convince Northerners that restoration of the Union would require the elimination of slavery and the participation of black soldiers. Southern political intransigence would demonstrate the futility of any negotiated settlement that would preserve slavery.

Chapter 5

Touched with Fire

The war profoundly affected the lives of everyone in the commonwealth. None was changed more, of course, than the soldiers who served in the Union army. Although no battles were fought on its soil, Massachusetts sent nearly 150,000 men to war. The backgrounds of Boston's soldiers reflected the diversity of its population. Soldiers included Harvard-educated grandsons of Revolutionary War Patriots, local craftsmen and merchants, newly arrived Irish immigrants and (starting in 1863) members of Boston's African American community. Their reasons for volunteering varied. Men enlisted to do their duty, preserve the Union, abolish slavery, earn steady pay and/or experience adventure. The Union army was formed from regiments provided by individual states. Massachusetts provided sixty-two regiments of infantry, five of cavalry, four of heavy artillery and sixteen of light artillery; nearly twenty thousand men served in the navy. Civil War army regiments typically included men from the same town or cluster of neighboring towns, but some regiments were organized according to ethnicity (e.g., Irish and black regiments).

The Civil War was the bloodiest war in U.S. history, and the carnage and suffering that occurred during its four long years are almost unimaginable. The war was fought with newly powerful and accurate weapons but old-fashioned tactics such as frontal attacks across open fields. Nearly fourteen thousand or over 8 percent of Massachusetts soldiers died, almost as many from disease as from mortal wounds; thousands more were wounded but survived. They were, as Oliver Wendell Holmes Jr. would reminisce decades later, members of a generation "touched with fire."

Left: Private Thomas Green of Company B, Eleventh Massachusetts Infantry Regiment. He was killed on August 29, 1862, at the Second Battle of Bull Run, Virginia. *Courtesy of the Library of Congress.*

Below: Brothers Private Henry Luther and First Sergeant Herbert E. Larrabee of Company B, Seventeenth Massachusetts Infantry Regiment. *Courtesy of the Library of Congress.*

Hub of the Second Revolution

Boston's Civil War soldiers were largely literate, and many wrote dozens of letters home. This book does not have the space to include all of their experiences, but what follows is a cross section of four of Boston's direct descendants of the generation that fought the American Revolution. (Boston's Irish and black soldiers will be discussed in Chapters 7 and 9, respectively, and the Emancipation Proclamation will be discussed in Chapter 8.) Their letters provide a range of views about the "rebellion" (as it was contemporaneously called), the Union and emancipation. In the brief sketches that follow, spelling and punctuation in quotations have been corrected as necessary to maintain the narrative flow.

Paul Joseph Revere

What better place to start but with the grandson and namesake of Patriot hero Paul Revere?[32] Revere, a twenty-nine-year-old married father of two, enlisted in the Union army during the summer of 1861 and was commissioned a major in the Twentieth Regiment Massachusetts Volunteer Infantry, nicknamed the "Harvard Regiment" because so many of the officers were students or graduates of the college. Paul Joseph Revere had entered Harvard in 1849 but was expelled for six months for "habitual disorderliness." After he returned, he graduated near the bottom of his class.

A sailing accident soon after graduation was credited with his rapidly gaining greater maturity. His father asked him to inspect copper mines in Minnesota, and while he was sailing on Lake Superior with four others, the sailboat capsized during a sudden tempest. Three of the

Lieutenant Colonel Paul Joseph Revere. *Courtesy of the Massachusetts Historical Society.*

men drowned, and the fourth maintained that he owed his life to Revere. His mother recalled, "[H]is careless youth was left behind...[He was now] keenly alive to the solemn realities of his being, or the obligations laid upon him to accomplish the work for which he had been spared."[33]

In December 1860, shortly before war began, poet and Cambridge resident Henry Wadsworth Longfellow published "The Midnight Ride of Paul Revere" in the *Atlantic Monthly*. Longfellow, an abolitionist and close friend of Charles Sumner, wrote to remind Northerners of the bravery of their Patriot ancestors and to awaken them as the "fate of the nation" again hung in the balance:[34]

> *And so through the night went his cry of alarm*
> *To every Middlesex village and farm,*
> *And a word that shall echo for evermore!*
> *For, borne on the night-wind of the past,*
> *Through all our history to the last,*
> *In the hour of darkness and peril and need,*
> *The people will waken and listen to hear*
> *The hurrying hoof-beats of that steed,*
> *And the midnight message of Paul Revere.*

When Paul Revere's grandson enlisted in July 1861, he wrote: "I have weighed it all; and there is something higher still. The institutions of the country, indeed free institutions throughout the world, hang on this moment. I should be ashamed of myself if I were to sit down in happy indulgence, and leave such a great matter as this to take its course." His elder brother, Edward Hutchinson Robbins Revere, a graduate of Harvard College and its medical school, also enlisted; he served as an assistant surgeon in the Twentieth Regiment.

Following training at Camp Readville in the Hyde Park neighborhood of Boston, the Twentieth Regiment departed for Washington, D.C., in August 1861. Arriving by train in Baltimore, the troops traveled on foot across the city, along the same route the Sixth Regiment had traveled in April on the eighty-sixth anniversary of Revere's grandfather's famous ride. Many who made this journey to the nation's capital would not return. The Twentieth Regiment would sustain the fifth-highest number of casualties of all Union regiments.

The Twentieth Regiment fought at Ball's Bluff on October 21, 1861. Union troops crossed the Potomac River into Virginia to raid what they believed to be an unguarded Confederate camp. Instead, the Union troops encountered a Confederate regiment. Seeking to rout the "rebs," more Union troops were sent across the river. However, the Union forces were outgunned, and many were stranded on the southern bank of the Potomac during their hasty retreat. "The river was now full of men who were drowning and shouting for help; but there was no help to give them except from God," wrote survivor Caspar Crowninshield to his mother.[35] The battle was a crushing Union defeat; nearly 500 men were killed, wounded or missing, and over 500 men, including both Reveres, were captured by the Confederates. (The Confederate casualties were fewer than 160.) The Twentieth regiment suffered 88 casualties, including 13 of its 22 officers.

Among those killed was William Lowell Putnam, whose family lore credited his grandfather, John Lowell, with drafting the Massachusetts Constitution's promise of equality that was relied upon by Mum Bett and Quock Walker in their eighteenth-century lawsuits to end slavery in Massachusetts. Six days before the battle, Putnam wrote a letter reflecting his strong abolitionist impulses:

> *He who said that a century of civil war is better than a day of slavery was right. God grant that every river in this land of ours may run with blood, and every city be laid in ashes rather than that this war should come to an end without the utter destruction of every vestige of this curse so monstrous. Human being never drew sword in a better cause than ours.*[36]

Revere was sent to the Confederate capital of Richmond, Virginia, where he and several other officers were confined in a cell normally occupied by convicted felons. From prison, Revere wrote to his wife, "You know with what feelings I undertook my military life and I can assure you that my experience thus far has been to confirm the opinion that I was merely fulfilling a duty." While imprisoned, Revere witnessed brutal beatings of "recalcitrant" slaves in the prison yard. After this experience, Revere embraced the abolitionist cause. He wrote that "the war of Rebellion was a war for the supremacy or extermination of human slavery…the institution of slavery was the salient point of the Rebellion."

The Union was at the time holding several Confederate sailors from the ship *Savannah* under a charge of piracy. To pressure the Federal government to release them, the Confederacy threatened to treat its newly won prisoners as criminals. As part of a negotiated settlement, the Federal government ultimately agreed to treat the Southern privateers as prisoners of war, and the Revere brothers were released.

Revere subsequently fought with the Twentieth Regiment at the Battle of Fair Oaks and the Seven Days Battle in the summer of 1862. After surviving a bout of malaria, he led his men at the Battle of Antietam on September 17, 1862. On that day, the bloodiest day in American history, Union forces turned back the Confederacy's attempt to invade Maryland. Revere's brother was mortally wounded as he performed surgery on an injured soldier in an exposed position at the rear of the regiment's lines. Revere returned to Boston to bury his brother and recover from an injury of his own, rejoining the regiment in the spring of 1863, when he was promoted to colonel and put in command. He found it hard to reconcile the contrast between life in Boston and that on the front, writing, "Could New England people realize what war really is, as shown in the experiences of those who inhabit the actual theatre of the war, they would hardly think and speak as flippantly of its operations as they are in the habit of doing."

Revere's final battle was Gettysburg. The Twentieth Regiment came under intense fire on July 2, 1863, the second day of the three-day battle, and many men lay flat on the ground, hoping to survive. Witnesses reported that Revere moved about his men, comforting both the living and the dying. He was fatally injured when a shell fragment lacerated a lung. He lived for two days, long enough to learn of the Union victory. Revere was buried next to his brother at Cambridge's Mount Auburn Cemetery. His mother wrote in her journal, "They knew the risk they ran. But the conflict must be met. It was their duty to aid it. The claim on them was as strong as on any and gallantly they answered it."[37]

Austin Clark Wellington

The boys when they enlisted ought to have known that it would be theirs not to reason why, theirs but to do and die.

Austin Clark Wellington, a private serving with the Thirty-eighth Regiment Massachusetts Volunteer Infantry, quoted these famous words from Alfred, Lord Tennyson's "Charge of the Light Brigade" soon after enlisting.[38] Like Revere, Wellington was a descendant of a Revolutionary Patriot: his great-grandfather Timothy Wellington fought against the redcoats on the Lexington Green in 1775. After finishing high school, Austin Wellington spent six years as an apprentice bookkeeper to Boston flour merchant Samuel Bowdlear before enlisting in August 1862 at the age of twenty-two. For the next three years, Wellington and Bowdlear exchanged frequent letters.

Following training at a camp in North Cambridge, Wellington spent his first months of service encamped near Baltimore. Preparing for battle, he wrote that his regiment "shall strike somewhere and we shall do all we can to sustain the reputation of Massachusetts soldiers." At the end of 1862, Wellington's regiment was ordered to Port Hudson, Louisiana. While en route, he saw plantations and slave dwellings for the first time, describing them as "quite a curiosity." He also reflected on the importance of his service to "sustain the nation's cause, and help vindicate the rights of free speech, free labor, and gain subjugation over the most wicked foe that ever engaged in warfare."

For nearly fifty days during May, June and July 1863, 7,500 heavily fortified Confederates fought to retain control of the Mississippi River. They resisted repeated charges from nearly 40,000 Union soldiers, including Wellington's regiment, under the command of Major General Nathaniel P. Banks, a former governor of Massachusetts. On May 29, Wellington described one such charge:

> *The first line had gone forward with a yell and then came the bullets. Forward second line, and immediately we found ourselves going forward into the very jaws of death. The men fell by the dozen, the ground seemed as if it was being ploughed, so thick came the hail. The artillery was at work "right smartly," and now and then it would speak forth with redoubled fury. We went forward until a large number had fallen, the General included, and were close on the works, when a lull came, we could do more, we had met with a repulse.*

Wellington's regiment suffered ninety-two casualties.

Wellington's belief that lives had been wasted led him to harshly criticize the tactics of his commanders: "As I look at it now, it was a poorly contrived scheme. Instead of causing the men to charge forward across an open field…a large force could have gone forward through ravines, under cover of darkness, and got very near the works, and thus have avoided the disaster which attended us in going across the field."

Despite General Banks's failings, Wellington remained committed to fighting against that "band of conspirators" who sought to "upset the liberties emanating from our glorious republic." "When such is the case," he

This photograph was contained in a letter Austin Clark Wellington sent to Samuel G. Bowdlear in 1863. Wellington expected Bowdlear to recognize him and provided no other identifying information. This photograph is contained in the Samuel G. Bowdlear and Austin C. Wellington Correspondence at the Boston Public Library. *Courtesy of the Boston Public Library.*

continued, "I will abolish all fear and dread and go to the rescue of that 'torn and battered' flag, the symbol of said republic."

Reporting on the state's success in filling two black regiments in 1863, Bowdlear wrote, "So you see your good old state is ahead in the matter of getting colored men to help fight the Rebs, and she is in fact ahead in almost everything connected with the war." Wellington replied, "It is encouraging to see them jump at the opportunity now given, to fight for their freedom."

Wellington remained in Louisiana until the fall of 1864, when his regiment was ordered to Alexandria, Virginia. He reported great relief leaving "the land of yellow fever and alligators." He did not intend to reenlist when his three-year term of service was up but wrote that he would be willing to serve again should "the nation call once more for help." He added, "In such a case I trust there would be left within me a spark of patriotism which would kindle anew the fire of devotion, and bid me to the 'front again.'" The war ended before Wellington had to make that decision.

Before leaving Louisiana, Wellington visited an illiterate, white enlisted man from Mississippi, David Wesley Shattles, who had joined the Thirty-eighth Regiment in December 1863 and was dying of malaria. Because Wellington knew that returning Shattles's personal effects and the $300 enlistment bounty owed to his wife would be impossible during wartime, he arranged to have the money sent to his own father in Boston. He promised Shattles that it would be invested and returned (with interest) to his family after the war ended. A family descendant recounted to this author family lore, supported by census records, that before 1870, Wellington visited Mississippi and delivered Shattles's personal effects and $900 to his grateful widow and children. "[W]ith the money they bought land and acquired many hundreds of acres over the years and were very successful because of the inheritance," this descendant reported.[39]

After the war, Wellington joined his father in a business that became the successful Austin C. Wellington Coal Company. He was a member of the Massachusetts State Militia, a longtime leader in veterans' affairs and served as a state legislator.

OLIVER WENDELL HOLMES JR.

When the famous U.S. Supreme Court justice died at ninety-four in 1935, his closet contained two uniforms on which was pinned the following note: "These uniforms were worn by me in the Civil War and the stains upon them are my blood."[40]

Descended from a colonial governor of Massachusetts and related to many leading Bostonians, Holmes was the son of Dr. Oliver Wendell Holmes Sr., an esteemed physician, poet and public intellectual who coined the terms "Boston Brahmin" to describe Boston's upper class and "hub of the solar system" to describe Bostonians' view of their city. Dr. Holmes was a devoted Unionist, and his wife, Amelia Lee Jackson, opposed slavery.

This photograph of Lieutenant Colonel Oliver Wendell Holmes Jr. was taken on January 2, 1864. *Courtesy of Harvard Law School Library, Historical & Special Collections.*

When the war began, Holmes was a Harvard College senior. His closest friend was Norwood Penrose Hallowell, a Quaker and ardent abolitionist from Philadelphia. Holmes had been raised with a strong sense of duty, and his friendship with Hallowell had deepened Holmes's abolitionist sentiments. He was among the young men who served as bodyguards to his cousin Wendell Phillips in the months after Lincoln's election when anxious conservatives harassed and harangued abolitionists. In the summer of 1861, Holmes and Hallowell were among the many Harvard students and graduates who volunteered for the Twentieth Regiment. Holmes was commissioned a first lieutenant in Company A and, following training—and a brief return to Harvard to take exams and receive a diploma—left Massachusetts in September 1861.

Following the defeat at Ball's Bluff, Holmes wrote to his parents of the slaughter—and of his behavior under fire:

> *From a third to half our company killed, wounded, and* [taken] *prisoner. Only eight officers of 22 in our Regiment got home unhurt.* [I] *did my duty handsomely…I was out in front of our men encouraging 'em on when a spent shot knocked the wind out of me and I fell—then I crawled to the rear a few paces…but I felt I couldn't* [go to the rear] *without more excuse so I got up and rushed to the front.*

Holmes recovered from this wound and, in March 1862, returned to his regiment, where he was commissioned a captain. After seeing action in the Battle of Fair Oaks, his regiment fought at Antietam in September. He was again wounded and wrote to his parents:

> [A] *ball entered at the rear passing straight through the central seam of coat and waistcoat collar coming out towa*[rd] *the front on the left side—yet it don't seem to have smashed my spine or I suppose I should be dead or paralyzed or something. It's more than 24 hours and I have remained pretty cocky, only of course feverish at times and some sharp burning pain in* [my] *left shoulder.*

Holmes asked his parents not to come to escort him home, but by the time his letter arrived, his father had already left Boston. Dr. Holmes described his frantic hunt for his son in an essay he published in the *Atlantic Monthly*. While searching near Frederick, Maryland, Dr. Holmes saw the road "filled with straggling and wounded soldiers…It was a pitiable sight, truly pitiable, yet so fast, so far beyond the possibility of relief…[B]oys flushed with fever, pale with exhaustion or haggard with suffering, dragged their weary limbs along…At the road side sat or lay others, quite spent with their journey."

Hub of the Second Revolution

After following several false leads, Dr. Holmes boarded a train carrying his son. He wrote, "[I]n the first car, on the fourth seat to the right, I saw my Captain…'How are you, Boy?' 'How are you, Dad?' Such are the proprieties of life, as they are observed among us Anglo-Saxons of the nineteenth century [even while] the hidden cisterns of the soul may be filling fast with sweet tears."

Holmes again recovered from his injuries and returned to his regiment. His subsequent letters display doubt about the Union's ability to win: "I've pretty much made up my mind that the South have achieved their independence & am almost ready to hope spring will see an end…believe me, we never shall lick 'em."

The following month, after the crushing Union defeat at Fredericksburg (Holmes had dysentery and missed that battle), he reiterated his doubt in "our success by arms" and displayed a young man's distrust of the wisdom of his elders: "I think in that matter I have better chances of judging than you…[who don't] realize the unity or the determination of the South. I think you are hopeful because (excuse me) you are ignorant."

Holmes was wounded for a third time at the Battle of Chancellorsville on May 3, 1863. This time he was hit in the heel and wrote, "I've been chloroformed & had bone extracted—probably shant lose foot." After recuperating, Holmes returned to active duty and accepted an invitation to join the staff of General Horatio Wright. Holmes wrote in May 1864 that he did not plan to reenlist at the end of his three years of service: "I have felt for some time that I didn't any longer believe in this being a duty. I started in this thing a boy—I am now a man and I have been coming to the conclusion for the last six months that my duty has changed…I have laboriously and with much suffering of mind and body earned the right…to decide for myself how I can best do my duty." In his next letter, Holmes reiterated, "[I have earned the] right to decide for myself how I can best do duty to my country."

Holmes returned to Boston in July 1864 and entered Harvard Law School. He became a professor there and served as chief justice of the Massachusetts Supreme Judicial Court before President Theodore Roosevelt appointed him to the U.S. Supreme Court. Justice Holmes's jurisprudence was shaped by his wartime experience. As historian Louis Menand wrote, "[Holmes] had gone off to fight because of his moral beliefs, which he held with singular fervor. The war did more than make him lose these beliefs. It made him lose his belief in beliefs. It impressed on his mind, in the most graphic and indelible way, a certain idea about the limits of ideas."[41] Holmes the idealist had metamorphosed into Holmes the realist and moral skeptic, who would reject intellectual absolutes, favor a free marketplace of ideas and famously write that the life of the law was based not on logic but on experience.

John Chase

"I am a strong union man. That is what I enlisted for was to restore the union, but I am not willing to shed one drop of blood to fight Slavery up or down. Let the niggers go to hell." So wrote John W. Chase[42] a few days after Lincoln issued the Emancipation Proclamation. Chase, who described himself as the most common of soldiers, could trace his American ancestors to 1640, and his grandfather fought in the American Revolution. An ardent Unionist, Chase maintained his anti-emancipation views throughout the war.

In August 1861, Chase was a cabinetmaker in Roxbury, a city annexed to Boston in 1868. A widower with four young children, he left them in the care of relatives and enlisted as a private in the First Massachusetts Battery Light Artillery. "I can truly say that if it needs my life to free my country from this Rebellion, I am willing to let it go," he wrote. A more prosaic reason would emerge later: "I always did despise the business [cabinetmaking] and never was contented when I worked at it and cannot bear the idea of ever going at it again."

Chase was promoted to corporal within two months, to sergeant in June 1863 and to first sergeant by that September. Prior to the end of his three-year term, Chase decided to reenlist. Despite seeing action at the bloody battlefields of Fredericksburg, Chancellorsville and Gettysburg, he managed to avoid serious injury or capture.

Chase wrote regularly to his brother, a carpenter, and 172 of those letters survive. They show his interest in news from home and his abiding interest in his children. Chase also frequently discussed the money he was able to save and send home as well as his desire for and appreciation of packages of food and clothing sent to him. Early on, Chase wrote, "They are drilling us now in dismounting the Guns and Carriages and it is a little more like work I tell you but I like it better and better every day. I never done anything yet that I like so well as I do Soldiering, but perhaps when we get into a fight I shall not like it so well but I feel as though I was ready for the devils."

Despite frustration with the lengthy encampment during the winter of 1861–62, Chase admired General George McClellan's commitment to preparation and training. Angry with those who accused McClellan of slowness to engage the Confederates, he wrote, "He is just the man to lead us to victory WHEN HE GETS READY."

Chase finally saw action during the Peninsula Campaign in the spring of 1862, when his regiment was engaged in a skirmish at West Point, Virginia. "I saw instances of courage that day that you would hardly believe," he wrote after the first skirmish. His regiment also fought at Antietam. "[A] good many of our brave boys were killed and a good many more wounded…The boys keep dropping off one by one and we miss a good many from the ranks that were with us one year ago today."

Sprinkled throughout his letters are Chase's occasional comments on blacks and abolitionists. Prior to the Emancipation Proclamation, Chase complained about the Union army's feeding and clothing "contrabands" (slaves who fled to Union army camps) with supplies he thought should be used for soldiers. On blacks serving in the army, Chase wrote on June 1, 1862, "God knows it is bad enough to be a Soldier without mixing ourselves up with niggers." After the Emancipation Proclamation, he wrote:

> *I don't feel as much like fighting as I used to for it looks to me as if fighting for the union and Constitution is played out and that now we are fighting for the Abolition of Slavery…I am not willing to shed one drop of blood to fight slavery up or down…and if a man wants to preach Abolition, Emancipation or any other ism, he must find somebody besides me to preach it to.*

In the election of 1864, Chase supported Democratic Party nominee McClellan for president. Just before the election, he wrote that he believed "the Lincoln Party is capable of anything that is mean to carry this election." Following Lincoln's reelection, he hoped the victors would "turn in earnest" to "putting down the rebellion," noting that it would be short work if the Republicans would be "half as much in earnest about it" as they were about the reelection campaign.

Chase's letters also reflected occasional disillusionment. Soon after the Union army experienced crushing defeats at Fredericksburg and Chancellorsville, he wrote, "I don't want to say anything harsh or wicked but I begin to think that this Soldiering is a damn big humbug or, to say the least, there is a good deal of humbug connected with it." But in

Massachusetts soldiers with a fifteen-inch Rodman cannon at Fort Warren. *Courtesy of the Boston Pubic Library.*

October 1863, Chase told his brother that he was thinking of reenlisting: "There is many things in [a] Soldier's life that I don't like and we have to put up with privations and hardships that we should get rid of in civil life, but then again there are things in it I do like."

Chase did reenlist. When his battery was dissolved after three years, he served with the Fifth Maine Battery and then the Ninth Massachusetts Battery. He arrived in Petersburg, Virginia, in the spring of 1865 just as the Union army mounted its final breakthrough attack after a lengthy

Hub of the Second Revolution

siege. Chase was mustered out on April 26, 1865. He returned to Roxbury and joined the Boston Police Department, where he served as a patrolman and eventually station captain.

This brief survey of a cross section of Boston's Revolutionary war offspring shows what happened when the ideals proclaimed before the war moved the hearts of men engaged in mortal combat. Each of the men profiled here had his life altered by the war. In his death, Revere became a hero like his grandfather; Wellington matured into a leader; Holmes transformed from an idealist to a realist; and Chase found a career that more resembled soldiering. For these men who experienced combat firsthand, the harsh lessons of killing never replaced their notions of gallantry and duty. As

Holmes said of these men, "The generation that carried on the war has been set apart by its experience. Through our great good fortune, in our youth our hearts were touched with fire. It was given to us to learn at the outset that life is a profound and passionate thing."[43]

Chapter 6

THE DAWN OF THE WOMEN'S RIGHTS REVOLUTION

On March 31, 1776, Abigail Adams wrote to her husband, John, who was in Philadelphia to attend the Continental Congress and debate the fate of the British colonies in America:

> *I long to hear that you have declared an independancy—and by the way, in the new Code of Laws which I suppose it will be necessary for you to make, I desire you would Remember the Ladies and be more generous and favourable to them than your ancestors…If perticuliar care and attention is not paid to the Ladies we are determined to foment a Rebellion, and will not hold ourselves bound by any Laws in which we have no voice or representation.*

Her request was unheeded, and women were granted no rights under either the U.S. Constitution or the Bill of Rights. When William Lloyd Garrison began to publish *The Liberator*, women still had few legal rights. But Boston's abolitionists would soon launch the women's rebellion that Adams had forecast.[44]

During the Second Great Awakening, religious leaders had encouraged women to participate in revival meetings and assume a primary role in their families' moral and spiritual improvement. Instilled with the ethical importance of good deeds, some women looked outward to contemplate the creation of a more perfect society. Slavery, which denied free agency and destroyed family bonds, was an obvious target of condemnation. Women could not fail to make the connection between the chains that bound slaves and the laws that bound themselves.

New England clergy soon regretted the revolution they had helped to unleash and sounded an alarm about women assuming a public role. When Sarah and Angelina Grimké departed on their 1837 public speaking tour throughout Massachusetts, Congregational Church clergy asserted in a widely disseminated pastoral letter that "[t]he power of woman is her dependence," and when she "assumes the place and tone of man as a public reformer…her character becomes unnatural." Lydia Maria Child retorted that women "have changed the household utensil to a living, energetic being, and [church leaders] have no spell to turn it into a broom again."[45]

In contrast to Protestant clergy, Garrison's radical vision included full equality for women. He welcomed them to the abolitionist crusade as equal partners, and women authors, agitators and organizers propelled the abolitionist movement forward. Boston women would make vital contributions not only to the triumph over slavery but also to the transformation of the role of women in American society.

In the years before the war began, the women's rights movement made considerable initial progress. In 1848, spurred on by their exclusion at an antislavery convention convened in London by British abolitionists, women abolitionists organized the groundbreaking Seneca Falls Convention to focus on women's rights and to join that effort with the antislavery campaign. This convention adopted the Declaration of Sentiments and Resolutions, modeled on the Declaration of Independence, which called for full legal and political rights for women. The success of the Seneca Falls Convention led to a series of national conventions (several in Massachusetts) during the 1850s.

When war began, the leaders of the women's rights movement agreed to suspend political advocacy for women's rights and to focus all their efforts on supporting the North and lobbying for emancipation of slaves. The war years nevertheless were vital in transforming the role of women in society. In addition to petitioning and advocating for emancipation, women served as nurses, created and led soldiers' aid societies, organized extensive networks of sewing circles, hosted sanitary fairs, worked in factories and managed farms and businesses. At least four hundred women disguised themselves as men and fought as soldiers. Massachusetts native Clara Barton, whose service as a Civil War nurse and relief organizer led to her founding the American Red Cross, remarked that the war years advanced women "at least fifty years…of the normal position which continued peace would have assigned her."[46] When the war ended, women were poised to demand, loudly

Hub of the Second Revolution

Our Women and the War. This lithograph is attributed to Winslow Homer and was published in *Harper's Weekly* on September 6, 1862. *Courtesy of the Boston Public Library.*

Women filling cartridges at the United States Arsenal in Watertown, Massachusetts. This Winslow Homer lithograph appeared on the cover of *Harper's Weekly* on July 20, 1861. *Courtesy of the Library of Congress.*

and persistently, entry into those spheres that were traditional bastions of male domination, including the voting booth and the legal profession.

As with the soldiers in the previous chapter, a cross section of Boston's women activists has been chosen: Maria Stewart, a black woman who inspired Boston's black community to attack racism and slavery; Lydia Maria Child, a white woman who wrote the first book-length attack on slavery and became an indefatigable author and reformer; Lucy Stone, the trailblazing founder of the American Woman Suffrage Association; Sarah Parker Remond, the Rosa Parks of Boston; Louisa May Alcott, the author and suffrage advocate; and Abigail Williams May, a brilliant manager and political leader.

Maria Stewart

In 1831, Garrison advertised for writings by black women to publish in his newly established newspaper. He later recalled, "You [Maria Stewart][47] made yourself known to me by coming into my office and putting into my hands for criticism and friendly advice a manuscript embodying your devotional thoughts and aspirations and also various essays pertaining to the condition of that class with which you were complexionally identified."[48]

Garrison was so impressed with Stewart's manuscript that he published *Religion and the Pure Principles of Morality: The Sure Foundation on Which We Must Build* as an independent pamphlet. In this essay, Stewart exclaimed, "All the nations of the earth are crying out for liberty and equality. Away, away with tyranny and oppression! And shall Africa's sons be silent any longer?"

She provided a brief and unadorned autobiography at the outset:

> *I was born in Hartford, Connecticut, in 1803; was left an orphan at five years of age; was bound out in a clergyman's family; had the seeds of piety and virtue early sown in my mind, but was deprived of the advantages of education, though my soul thirsted for knowledge. Left them at fifteen years of age; attended Sabbath schools until I was twenty; in 1826 was married to James W. Stewart; was left a widow in 1829; was, as I humbly hope and trust, brought to the knowledge of the truth, as it is in Jesus, in 1830; in 1831 made a public profession of my faith in Christ.*

During the next two years, Stewart gave four public addresses in Boston. The first was delivered to the African American Female Intelligence Society of America, established in 1831. There she introduced the themes to which she would return, urging women to become moral leaders of the black community and help its members ascend from the degraded conditions in which they lived. Stewart's themes echoed the society's own goals: "diffusion of knowledge, the suppression of vice and immorality, and cherishing such virtues as will render us happy and useful to society."

Stewart's second public lecture, to the New England Anti-Slavery Society, is considered the first of any American woman, black or white, delivered to an audience composed of men and women. She exhorted Boston's black community to take an active role in improving their own deplorable conditions by turning "their attention more assiduously to moral worth and intellectual improvement." Doing so, she promised, would lead to a decrease in racial prejudice, "and the whites would be compelled to say, unloose those fetters!"

In her third address, at the African Masonic Hall in February 1833, Stewart responded to those within the black community who had criticized her public role: "Had the men amongst us, who have had an opportunity, turned their attention as assiduously to mental and moral improvement as they have to gambling and dancing, I might have remained quietly at home, and they stood contending in my place." She also condemned the popular colonization movement and challenged its supporters to "expend the money which they collect in erecting a college to educate her injured sons in this land of gospel, light, and liberty." After again receiving withering criticism for speaking out, Stewart decided to leave Boston for New York. At her "Farewell Address" delivered on September 21, 1833, at the African Meeting House, Stewart challenged her critics: "What if I am a woman? Did [God] not raise up Deborah [,] Esther [and] Mary Magdalene?"

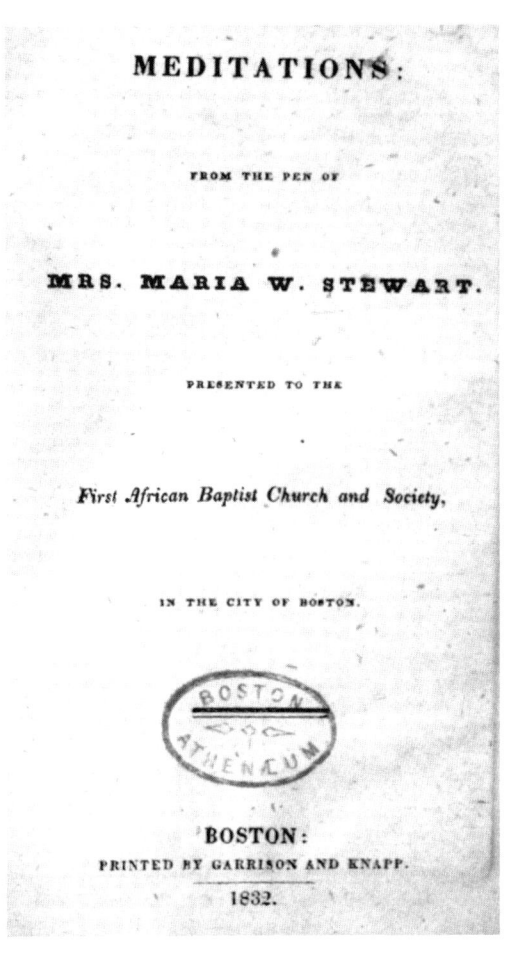

Cover of *Meditations from the Pen of Mrs. Maria Stewart*, published by Garrison & Knapp in 1832. Tract C225. *Courtesy of the Boston Athenaeum.*

Stewart never again spoke publicly on political issues, but her pathbreaking speeches opened the door for other women, such as the Grimké sisters, Sarah Remond and Lucy Stone, to become public antislavery lecturers. Stewart lived the remainder of her life as a virtual unknown in New York, Baltimore and Washington, D.C. She taught school, struggled with bitter poverty, privately supported abolitionist causes and, after the Civil War, became head of housekeeping at the Freedman's Hospital in Washington. After decades of silence, Stewart and Garrison again corresponded, and Stewart visited him in Boston in 1879. In a letter written shortly thereafter, Garrison expressed joy in the extraordinary "changes and experiences" in the nation since he and Stewart had first met, while also noting the long road that remained to end race-based inequality.

Lydia Maria Child

Over the river, and through the wood,
To grandfather's house we go;
The horse knows the way to carry the sleigh
Through the white and drifted snow.

Best remembered today for her nostalgic Thanksgiving Day poem, Lydia Maria Child[49] was an ardent abolitionist and activist as well as a leading woman of letters.

Born in the Boston suburb of Medford in 1802, the precocious Child wrote at age twenty her first historical novel, *Hobomok*, which portrayed Native Americans sympathetically. Two years later, she became the editor of the *Juvenile Miscellany* magazine, the nation's first children's magazine. In 1829, she married lawyer David Child, who would share her dedication to the abolitionist cause. Soon thereafter, she wrote *The Frugal Housewife*, a "self-help" book that offered practical budget tips on all aspects of housekeeping. She followed this successful publication with *The Mother's Book*, which offered detailed advice on rearing children.

When Child met Garrison in 1830, she decided to devote her literary talents to the abolitionist cause. Many decades later, Child remarked that Garrison "got hold of the strings of my conscience, and pulled me into Reforms. It is of no use to imagine what might have been if I had never met him."

Hub of the Second Revolution

Lydia Maria Child. *Courtesy of the Massachusetts Historical Society.*

In 1833, she wrote *An Appeal in Favor of That Class of Americans Called Africans*, the first book-length antislavery tract published in the United States. Tracing slavery's history, she described its pernicious effects on both slaves and slaveholders. Daringly, she also addressed the sexual subjugation of slave women, stating "it is indeed a strange state of society where the father sells his child and the brother puts his sister up at auction." Like Garrison, Child sought an end to slavery, opposed colonization and supported full equal rights for blacks. She wrote, "[A free black man], however intelligent, is not allowed to pursue any business more lucrative than that of a barber, a shoe-black, or a waiter…It is unjust that a man should, on account of his complexion, be prevented from performing more elevated uses in society."

While Garrison appreciated her efforts, most did not. The market for her other books dried up, and Child lost her post as editor of *Juvenile Miscellany*. Financial hardships ensued as David Child's repeated attempts to earn a living failed, and his indebtedness even briefly landed him in prison.

In 1841, Child took her literary talents to New York, where for two years she served as editor of the newly created *National Anti-Slavery Standard*. She also addressed the plight of women, which she called the result of the "animal instinct and brute force" on which men relied to govern the world. Child remained in New York, living apart from her husband, and resumed publishing works for children, including "Over the River and through the Wood," which first appeared in *Flowers for Children* (1844).

In 1849, Child and her husband returned together to Massachusetts, where she denounced the Fugitive Slave Act and the Kansas-Nebraska Act. In the wake of the caning of Charles Sumner, she wrote a short story, "The Kansas Emigrants," about peace-loving settlers from New England who move to Kansas and are tormented by border ruffians. Horace Greeley, the influential editor of the *New York Tribune*, interrupted his serialization of Charles Dickens's *Little Dorrit* to publish it.[50]

In 1859, Child publicly supported John Brown's unsuccessful raid at Harpers Ferry and wrote directly to Virginia governor Henry Wise to plead his case. When Wise retorted, "We have no sympathy with your sentiments of sympathy with Brown," Child replied with a blistering attack on slavery, which she called "an infringement of all law [that] adheres to no law, save for its own purposes of oppression."

In 1861, shortly before war commenced, Child edited and wrote the preface to self-emancipated slave Harriet Jacobs's autobiographical *Incidents in the Life of a Slave Girl*. Jacobs described her harrowing escape from slavery, which included her hiding in a ceiling crawl space in her grandmother's house for seven years. Child defended Jacobs's graphic description of the sexual abuse she was forced to endure, stating, "This peculiar phase of slavery has generally been kept veiled; but the public ought to be made acquainted with its monstrous features."

During the war, Child strongly advocated for the expansion of war aims to include emancipation. At its close, she published a book of inspirational readings designed for newly emancipated slaves. *The Freedmen's Book* related the accomplishments of black men and women, including Phillis Wheatley, Frederick Douglass and Ellen and William Craft. She went on to support rights for Native Americans and suffrage for blacks and women. When Child died in 1880, Wendell Phillips lauded her willingness to "die for a principle and starve for an idea."

Lucy Stone

Lucy Stone,[51] the first woman from Massachusetts to earn a college degree, lectured against slavery and for women's rights. Breaking many barriers, she spearheaded the first national women's rights convention, invented egalitarian wedding vows and kept her maiden name after marriage.

Stone was born in 1818 on a farm in West Brookfield, Massachusetts. While working as a schoolteacher in the late 1830s, she avidly followed debates over the "proper" role of women in the wake of the Grimkés' antislavery lecture tour. Stone decided to save her earnings and attend college. She enrolled at Oberlin, the nation's first coeducational college, in 1843. Soon she organized a debating society so female students could develop their oratorical skills. In the same vein, Stone declined an invitation to write a commencement speech because even progressive Oberlin would have required that a man publicly read her speech. By commencement, Stone had planned her future. She described her objectives to her mother: "I expect to plead not for the slave only, but for suffering humanity everywhere. Especially do I mean to labor for the elevation of my sex."

In 1848, Stone became a lecturer for the New England

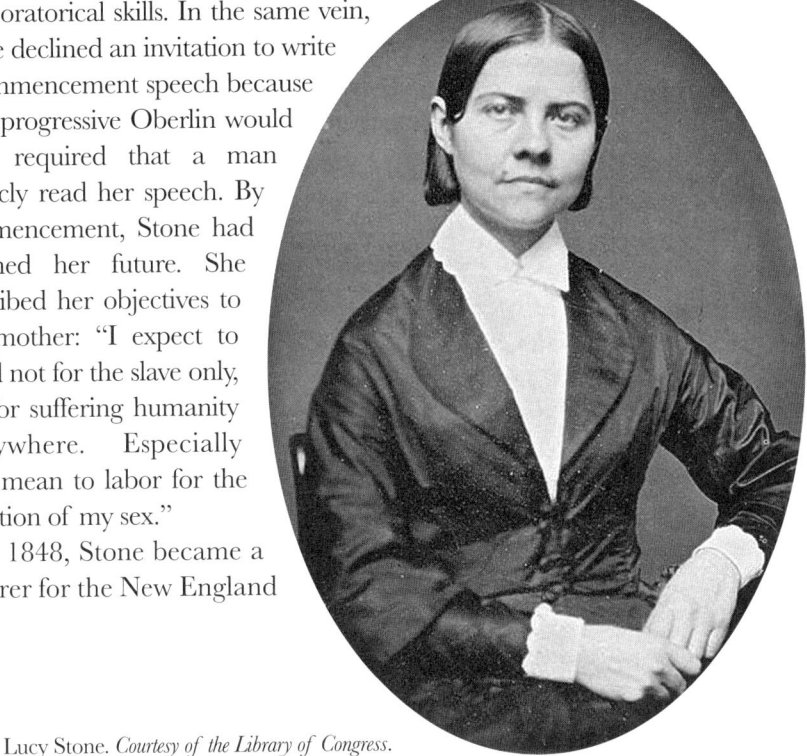

Lucy Stone. *Courtesy of the Library of Congress.*

Anti-Slavery Society, agreeing to a forward-thinking job arrangement. She would advocate for women's rights on weekdays and against slavery on weekends. She was an extraordinarily effective speaker; one early review described her manner as "gentle, calm, dignified, earnest," her voice "clear and sonorous," her gestures "natural and graceful" and her remarks cohesive with "beginning, middle, and end."[52]

Although Stone did not attend the Seneca Falls Convention in 1848, she was a chief organizer of the First National Women's Rights Convention, held in the central Massachusetts city of Worcester in 1850 and attended by nine hundred delegates from the Northern states. Stone advocated for the circulation of petitions seeking suffrage and the right of married women to hold property. Addressing the delegates, she announced, "We want to be something more than the appendages of Society…we want that when she dies, it may not be written on her grave-stone that she was the [widow] of somebody." The convention closed with a call "for the total reorganization of all social, political, industrial interests and institutions" and launched sustained momentum by appointing permanent committees to advocate on women's issues and plan annual conventions.

The Second National Women's Rights Convention also was held in Worcester, while the third was held in Syracuse, New York, in 1852. That convention was the first that Susan B. Anthony attended, and Stone's speech there is widely credited with persuading Anthony to devote her life to the cause of women's rights.

In 1855, Stone married radical abolitionist Henry Browne Blackwell. The couple agreed that Stone would continue to use her own name, that their wedding vows would omit any mention of the word "obey" and that they would protest all property and estate laws that favored the husband.

Stone suspended her advocacy for women's rights during the war. Although she made only a few public appearances, she joined with Anthony, Elizabeth Cady Stanton and others in 1863 to form the Women's National Loyal League. The league collected hundreds of thousands of signatures on petitions seeking a constitutional amendment to abolish slavery.

At the close of the war, Stone, Stanton, Anthony and Frederick Douglass were among those who formed the American Equal Rights Association to press for suffrage for both blacks and women. However, by 1869, association members were arguing over whether suffrage for blacks or women was a higher political priority. The proposed Fifteenth Amendment would grant suffrage to black men but not women. Frederick Douglass asserted, "I must say that I do not see how anyone can pretend that there is the same urgency in giving the ballot to women as to the Negro." Anthony bitterly countered that suffrage must be given "to the most intelligent first," an underhanded jibe at uneducated, newly freed blacks. Stone sided with Douglass and supported the Fifteenth Amendment, explaining, "There are two great oceans [of wrongs]; in one is the black man, and in the other is the woman." She continued, "I will be thankful in my soul if anybody can get out of the terrible pit."[53]

Anthony and Stanton left to form a new organization, the National Woman Suffrage Association, dedicated only to woman suffrage. Stone, her husband and Julia Ward Howe (the author of "Battle Hymn of the Republic"—see Chapter 8) founded the Boston-based American Woman Suffrage Association, which supported the Fifteenth Amendment as well as ongoing efforts in support of woman suffrage. Stone edited the association's weekly, the *Woman's Journal*, in an office located steps away from the Massachusetts State House.

In 1873, Stone led Boston's women activists in calling for a Centennial Tea Party rally in Faneuil Hall to protest "taxation without representation" and the continuing despotic power of men. Three thousand attended and heard from speakers including Stone, Julia Ward Howe, Frederick Douglass, William Lloyd Garrison and Wendell Phillips. Echoing the abolitionists, who had claimed that the treatment of slaves was far worse than the British treatment of the colonists, Stone proclaimed:

> *The wrong done to men a hundred years ago, by the government of England, bears no comparison to the injustice and wrong done to women by the government of this country to-day…O men of Massachusetts, how can we make you know that the injustice and wrong you are to-day doing to women is greater than that which your fathers resisted, and that it calls as loudly for repeal?*

When Massachusetts for the first time permitted women to vote in local elections for school committee members several years later, Stone declined because election officials insisted that she register as Lucy Stone Blackwell.

Relations between the National Woman Suffrage Association and the American Woman Suffrage Association were bitter until 1890, when a new generation of leaders, including Stone's daughter, Alice Stone Blackwell, engineered a reunification. Stone, Stanton and Anthony occupied the three primary leadership positions of the new National American Woman Suffrage Association. Stone was, however, in poor health and died three years later.

Sarah Parker Remond

More than one hundred years before Rosa Parks refused to give up her seat on an Alabama bus, Sarah Parker Remond[54] challenged segregated seating in a Boston theater. In 1853, a manager at the Howard Athenaeum called police to evict Remond, her sister and abolitionist William Nell when they refused to leave seats in a section reserved for whites. While forcefully removing Remond, the police injured her shoulder. She brought a civil action for damages, and a police court awarded her the sizable sum of $500 (about $14,000 in today's dollars).

Remond was born in 1826 in Salem, Massachusetts, to a free black family who valued education. Her father, John Remond, had a successful catering business. When the Salem public schools refused to allow the Remond children to attend the town's high school, her father placed them in an all-black private school and helped organize a boycott against school segregation. Bowing to pressure, the Salem school committee voted in 1844 to desegregate the town's schools. Remond later credited her parents with instilling in her a drive for learning and the strength "to meet the terrible pressure which prejudice against color would force upon me."

Remond's older brother, Charles Lenox Remond, became a highly regarded antislavery lecturer. He was the preeminent African American abolitionist orator until Frederick Douglass joined the lecture circuit. In 1843, Charles was the first black person to testify before a committee of the Massachusetts legislature. His testimony helped persuade the legislature to abolish segregation on railroad cars.

Sarah Remond's 1853 challenge to segregated seating at the Howard Athenaeum marked her emergence as an activist. In

Sarah Parker Remond. *Courtesy of the Massachusetts Historical Society.*

1856, at age thirty, she joined her brother as a lecturer on an antislavery tour of five states, including Massachusetts. In 1858, she attended the annual women's rights convention in New York. That same year, abolitionist leaders asked her to travel to Great Britain to help rally overseas support for the North if war came. While in England, Remond stayed for a time with Ellen and William Craft and continued her education at Bedford College in London. In England, Ireland and Scotland, Remond's speeches highlighted the predicament of slave women and distinguished their state from that of Britain's poor. "There was this measurable difference between the condition of the poorer English women and that of the slave woman—that their persons were free and their progeny their own, while the slave woman was the victim of the heartless lust of her master, and the children whom she bore were his property."[55]

When the Civil War began, Remond continued her efforts to sway British public opinion against the Confederacy. Later in the war, she wrote a pamphlet titled *The Negroes as Freedmen and Soldiers*, which publicized in England the services rendered by newly freed slaves as soldiers. After the war, she moved to Italy, where she studied medicine and became a midwife and physician. She never returned to the United States and died in Rome in 1894.

Louisa May Alcott

Louisa May Alcott,[56] the author of *Little Women*, lived much of her life in Boston, although she wrote her most famous novel while living in suburban Concord. Her house is a stone's throw from where Minutemen had, in 1775, fired the "shot heard 'round the world." Alcott's parents, Bronson Alcott and Abigail May, were reformers and abolitionists. Her mother, who was related to early Garrisonians Samuel E. Sewall and Samuel Joseph May, was a pioneering social worker; her father was an idealistic educator who founded a progressive school and a short-lived utopian community. Their home was a stop on the Underground Railroad, a loosely organized secret network of escape routes and safe houses utilized by self-emancipated slaves.

In the same spirit, Alcott attended sermons of radical abolitionist Theodore Parker at Boston's Music Hall. She recorded in her journal in 1856: "Go to hear Parker, and he does me good. Asks me to come Sunday evenings to his house. I did go there, and met [Wendell] Phillips, [William

Lloyd] Garrison…and other great men…" Of the execution of John Brown in 1859, she noted, "The execution of Saint John the Just took place on the second [of December]."

The unmarried Alcott wrote the following in her journal on November 29, 1862, her birthday: "Thirty years old. Decided to go to Washington as nurse if I could find a place. Help needed, and I love nursing, and must let out my pent-up energy in some new way." Superintendent of Nurses Dorothea Dix required all volunteer nurses to be at least thirty. Dix was herself another Massachusetts pioneer; before the war, she had dedicated herself to advocating for humane treatment for the mentally ill.

Alcott wrote to Hannah Stevenson, the first volunteer nurse from Massachusetts, and soon thereafter, Alcott reported for duty at Union

Louisa May Alcott. *Courtesy of the Boston Public Library.*

Hospital in Georgetown, just outside Washington, D.C. She served for only several weeks before contracting typhoid fever and returning home. While recuperating, Alcott revised her journal entries and letters home into a collection of short pieces that she titled *Hospital Sketches*.

The book depicts the experiences of a fictional nurse, Tribulation Periwinkle. On her first morning of service, Periwinkle described her initial shock at being asked to wash the wounded men:

> *If she had requested me to shave them all, or dance a hornpipe on the stove funnel, I should have been less staggered...However, there was no time for nonsense, and, having resolved when I came to do everything I was bid, I drowned my scruples in my wash-bowl, clutched my soap manfully, and, assuming a business-like air, made a dab at the first dirty specimen I saw.*

Speaking through Periwinkle, Alcott described assisting with dressing wounds and amputations. One doctor asked her to tell a soldier he would die because "women have a way of doing such things comfortably." She also conveyed the poignancy of helping dying soldiers write their final letters home. *Hospital Sketches* brought Alcott notice as a writer while drawing the North's attention to the plight of sick and wounded soldiers.

After the war, Alcott became one of the most beloved authors of the second half of the nineteenth century. *Little Women*, which is set during the war years, was published in 1868. She also strongly supported woman suffrage, working hard to move people "out of the old ruts." When Massachusetts permitted women to vote in school committee elections in 1879, Alcott was the first woman to register in Concord. Of casting her vote, she related, "No bolt fell on our audacious heads, no earthquake shook the town."[57] In her final novel, *Jo's Boys* (1886), young men resistant to woman suffrage speak what Alcott characterized as "feeble, vulgar twaddle."

Abigail Williams May

Abigail Williams May[58] was a leader in the postwar suffrage movement. Born in Boston in 1829, May grew up in a family that supported Boston's abolitionists. She copied excerpts of Parker's sermons in her daily journal, and her cousins included abolitionists Samuel Joseph May and Louisa May Alcott. In 1861, soon after the war began, May joined the New England

Women's Auxiliary Association, the Boston branch of the United States Sanitary Commission. The Sanitary Commission was created to help organize women's volunteer efforts to raise funds to provide medical and other supplies to sick and wounded soldiers. The commission was, however, led by men who, among other discriminatory gestures, undermined Dorothea Dix's efforts to oversee training and placement of Northern nurses.

May began as the secretary of the executive committee of the New England Women's Auxiliary Association, one of twelve regional branches of the Sanitary Commission. She became regional branch chair in 1862, a position she retained throughout the war. May's organizational and managerial skills were legendary. "She had a very remarkable power of controlling and inspiring and converting," recalled a co-worker.[59] She also designed an effective and decentralized system of associate managers to act as liaisons between the regional branch and its many local affiliates in towns throughout the region. During her tenure, the New England Women's Auxiliary Association grew to include over one thousand local aid societies that collectively raised over $1 million. Holding sanitary fairs (with exhibitions, parades and speeches) was a very successful fundraising technique; a fair held in Boston during 1863 raised nearly $150,000.

Roxbury women sewing for the troops. *Courtesy of the Boston Public Library.*

The wartime work of May and her colleagues provided "critical experience in aligning politically prominent men to a woman's cause and in manipulating a male-run bureaucracy."[60] After the war, these politically savvy women would use their skills in support of woman suffrage. May founded the New England Women's Club and served as president of the New England Woman Suffrage Association, whose membership overlapped with that of the American Woman Suffrage Association led by Lucy Stone. During the 1870s, May spearheaded support for a law—ultimately enacted in 1879—that allowed women to vote for local school committees. Even before she could vote for that office, May ran for and won a seat on the Boston School Committee, although the other committee members initially refused to seat her. In 1879, she became the first woman appointed to the Massachusetts state board of education.

Despite this progress and the best efforts of the generation of abolitionist-activists, the struggle for suffrage in Massachusetts would drag on for several decades more. As late as 1915, Massachusetts' voters (all of whom were, of course, male) defeated a proposed woman suffrage amendment to the Massachusetts Constitution. Women's right to vote was not attained until 1920, when the Nineteenth Amendment to the U.S. Constitution was finally adopted.

Chapter 7

THE FIGHTING IRISH

The influx of immigrants from the Emerald Isle would make their own contributions in Civil War Boston. A small Irish community had existed in Boston during the late eighteenth century, and a steady stream of immigrants flocked to the city during the first decades of the nineteenth century. By 1830, seven thousand Irish immigrants, mostly Protestants from the Ulster area, lived in the city of sixty-one thousand. The Irish potato famine, which began in 1845 and lasted into the 1850s, led to a flood of Irish immigrants. These newcomers were essentially all Catholic, and most were desperately poor. By 1855, fifty thousand Irish-born immigrants (and children of the Irish-born) made up over one-third of the city's population. Raised to believe in order, obedience and hierarchy, Boston's Irish were fiercely loyal to their adopted country, and most were conservative in their politics. Unskilled and uneducated, these new immigrants competed for menial jobs against native-born white laborers and members of Boston's small black community.

Boston's Irish Catholics confronted widespread discrimination. The Protestant majority—most of whom had English ancestors—typically greeted these new arrivals with hostility. Prejudice against Catholics had "seemingly been transported to Boston with the pilgrims and the Puritans."[61] Many Protestant Bostonians harbored stereotypes of the Irish as a lazy, drunken and violent people.[62] Meager earnings forced most Irish to live in squalor where disease was rampant, reinforcing these stereotypes. "No Irish Need Apply" appeared on signs on shop windows and factory doors throughout the city. Lyman Beecher, a Presbyterian minister and father of Harriet Beecher Stowe, accused the Catholic religion of opposing Republican values. In the wake of his remarks, a Protestant mob burned down the Ursuline Convent, a Roman Catholic convent and school in Charlestown (today a part of Boston). Abolitionist Theodore Parker lamented that the large number of Irish were turning Boston into the "Dublin of America."

The Irish community eschewed the antislavery movement into the 1850s even as many native-born Bostonians flocked to the Free Soil Party. Several factors drove this opposition to abolitionism. Many Irish dreaded economic insecurity, given the prospect that freed slaves would come north and compete for unskilled jobs. Others felt stark racism. Nor did the Irish have much patience for the abolitionist claim that slavery violated a "higher law." Patrick Donahoe, the publisher of *The Pilot*, Boston's widely read and influential Irish-Catholic newspaper,[63] accused abolitionists of seeking to make "constitutions and laws subservient to the will, or the passions of individuals—to emancipate man from all law, all restraint [and declaring] that the decrees of government are to be disobeyed, and that the decisions of courts are to be trampled upon." The result of this "insane radicalism" would, he predicted, be "wild anarchy." Many Irish also viewed abolitionism as a plot hatched by the despised English to undermine the growing economic and political power of the United States. As early as 1842, *The Pilot* warned:

> *We cannot doubt that England gloats upon the prospect of a rupture between the Northern and Southern divisions of this Republic. She contemplates with proud satisfaction the evidences that point to this fearful wreck of the patriot's hope, and zealously does she stir the cauldron of enmities in order to accelerate the fall of the people's power. She dreads the potent influence of this country in tearing up the foundations of monarchical government.*

Steeped in tradition, hierarchy and hatred of the English, Boston's Irish generally concluded that slavery was an institution protected by both custom and the Constitution and that its opponents were unpatriotic rabble-rousers.

The Anthony Burns case in 1854 powerfully illustrates the divide between the Irish and antislavery communities. Members of the local Irish Catholic Columbian Artillery, a volunteer militia led by Captain Thomas Cass, were among those escorting Burns on his journey from the courthouse to the harbor, guarding against any attempted rescue by the hordes of angry onlookers. *The Pilot* denounced the crowd supporting Burns as anarchists and applauded the role of the Columbian Artillery in returning him to his rightful owner. *The Pilot* also supported that year's Kansas-Nebraska Act and the right of Southern slaveholders to take their "property" with them into new territories.

Following the 1854 state elections, which swept members of the nativist Know Nothing Party to power (see Chapter 3), a series of new laws were enacted that targeted Irish immigrants. One required the disbanding of all militia companies composed of immigrants (e.g., the Columbian Artillery), while another mandated the reading of the Protestant Bible in public schools. A new state constitutional amendment required that new citizens reside in the country for two years after naturalization before becoming eligible to vote. The rise of the Know Nothings strengthened the ties between Irish immigrants and the Democratic Party. The Democrats were conservative on the issue of slavery but were generally pro-immigrant and worked to build a loyal base among new citizens. The Irish thus became the political allies of those merchants and manufacturers who sought to preserve the status quo between the North and the South.

In the election of 1856, the Irish strongly supported Democratic Party presidential nominee James Buchanan against Republican candidate John Fremont. The Irish perceived Republicans, often correctly, as the party of former "Know Nothings," with hearts "as soft as butter towards the colored laborer of the South, but hard as flint towards a large portion of the white laborers."

As the Republican Party became dominant in Massachusetts during the late 1850s, the loyalties of Boston's Irish stayed firmly rooted in the Democratic Party. To many Irish, John Brown's raid at Harpers Ferry symbolized the abolitionist disregard for law and order, and *The Pilot* condemned his actions. In the election of 1860, Donahoe urged his readers to vote for Democrat Stephen Douglas rather than Republican Abraham Lincoln. Donahoe harshly criticized gubernatorial candidate John Albion Andrew, whom he called a member of the "fanatical 'John Brown clique of Republicans.'"[64] *The Pilot* again connected the Republicans to the despised Know Nothings and claimed that every vote for a Republican was a vote for the constitutional amendment denying foreigners the vote for two years after naturalization.[65] Over 70 percent of Boston's eligible Irish voters in 1860 opposed Lincoln,[66] and Irish votes were instrumental in electing Democrat Joseph Wightman as mayor of Boston. In contrast to Andrew's preparations for war, Wightman advocated in his inaugural for the "restor[ation] of harmony in federal relations" and the taking of "conciliatory measures" to protect the Union.

Rally 'Round the Flag

The secession of Southern states changed the picture for Boston's Irish. They felt that Southern secessionists had betrayed the nation and that the North was committed to its preservation. The Irish "did not vote for Mr. Lincoln but they will support the Constitution," announced *The Pilot*. With the issue of slavery temporarily sidelined, the Irish rallied to "stand by the Union; fight for the Union; die by the Union." When Lincoln called for troops to suppress "the rebellion," Donahoe saw an opportunity to prove Irish patriotism and pledged to lead efforts to finance the raising of an Irish regiment. Governor Andrew gave permission to forty-year-old Thomas Cass, the former commander of the (disbanded) Columbia Artillery, to organize the Ninth Regiment Massachusetts Volunteer Infantry, which would be composed of Irishmen.

Colonel Thomas Cass, commander of the Ninth Regiment Massachusetts Volunteer Infantry, which was nicknamed the "Fighting Irish." *Courtesy of the Library of Congress.*

The ranks of the Ninth Regiment filled quickly as men responded to the opportunity to fight for the Union—and to receive steady pay. Many of these new recruits were former members of the Columbian Artillery. On June 25, 1861, Governor Andrew presented the regiment with the U.S., Massachusetts and regimental flags. The last was an amalgamation of Irish and American symbols. One side included an American coat of arms and an Irish flag, while the other contained an Irish harp with red, white and blue strings. The flag proclaimed: "As aliens and strangers thou didst us befriend. As sons and true patriots we do thee defend." Standing in front of the Massachusetts State

Hub of the Second Revolution

Detail from an illustration showing recruitment for the Ninth Regiment on Flagstaff Hill in Boston Common. Boston's Civil War monument stands on Flagstaff Hill. *Courtesy of the Boston Public Library.*

House, Governor Andrew told the members of the regiment and the large crowd that "the United States knows no distinction between its native-born citizens and those born in other countries."[67]

In July 1861, Governor Andrew asked President Lincoln for permission to raise ten additional regiments in Massachusetts, including another Irish regiment. When permission was granted, Donahoe again led efforts to finance what would become the Twenty-eighth Regiment. After it departed from Boston in January 1862, the Twenty-eighth joined Irish regiments from New York and Pennsylvania to form the Irish Brigade. Boston bishop John Fitzpatrick successfully insisted that a Catholic chaplain accompany the Twenty-eighth Regiment and join the Ninth Regiment.[68]

The Ninth Regiment was heavily engaged in the Peninsula Campaign, where, for five bloody months during the spring and summer of 1862, General George McClellan sought unsuccessfully to capture the Confederate capital of Richmond. The Ninth Regiment endured over two hundred casualties, and its bravery earned it the moniker "the fighting Irish." Recalling the Battle of Gaines Mill on June 27, 1862, during which the regiment tried to hold a bridge under attack, Sergeant Daniel MacNamara wrote that men fell dead and wounded "like grain before the reaper's sickle."[69] Colonel Cass was mortally wounded leading his men at the Battle of Malvern Hill on July 1, 1862. Colonel Patrick Robert Guiney, his replacement, was unusual among the Irish solders he led. A well-educated Irish immigrant, he was a lawyer who opposed slavery and belonged to the Republican Party.[70]

As part of the Irish Brigade, the Twenty-eighth Regiment fought in several of the war's largest and best-known battles, including Fredericksburg, Chancellorsville and Gettysburg. The Irish Brigade had the third-highest number of battlefield casualties of any Union brigade. At Fredericksburg in December 1862, it suffered a staggering casualty rate of nearly 40 percent. Private Peter Welsh described a futile frontal assault against Confederates shielded behind a stone wall on a hill. Confederate artillery "mow[ed] whole gaps out of our ranks. Every man that was near me in the right of the company was killed or wounded except one."[71]

After Fredericksburg and a long winter of encampment and hardship, the survivors of Boston's Irish regiments decided to celebrate St. Patrick's Day. The Ninth Regiment organized a series of events, including a sack race, climbing a greased pole, jumping matches and horse racing. As always during the war, death was ever present—the regiment's quartermaster died during a horse race. The Irish Brigade hosted a large celebration, and men from different corps joined in the games, dancing and feasting.[72] Soldier

Men of the Ninth Regiment and their chaplain prepare to celebrate Mass at Camp Cass, Virginia. *Courtesy of the Library of Congress.*

Peter Welsh was appointed to serve as color-bearer, writing to his wife, "I shall feel proud to bear up that flag of green, the emblem of Ireland…and especially to having received it on that day dear to every Irish heart, the festival of St. Patrick."[73]

The heroism and sacrifice of Boston's Irish troops had a marked effect on the prejudices of the Protestant majority. On July 4, 1861, Boston for the first time raised Ireland's flag on Boston Common during the annual Independence Day celebration. The Massachusetts legislature repealed anti-Irish legislation enacted by the Know Nothing legislature and approved the charter of a Jesuit school, Boston College. The Massachusetts Constitution was again amended in 1863, this time to expunge the amendment that had required a naturalized citizen to wait two years to vote after becoming eligible.[74] When Harvard University bestowed an honorary doctorate in divinity upon Bishop Fitzpatrick, *The Pilot* described the act as "public evidence of a waning of the prejudice against our religion coming from the highest range of Protestant society."[75]

THE EMANCIPATION PROCLAMATION

To replenish the decimated regimental ranks, Boston's Irish community recruited heavily during the late summer and fall of 1862 and offered a long list of reasons, both lofty and practical, for enlisting. These included proving oneself a worthy inheritor of the "indomitable valor and bravery which distinguished [their] ancestors on many a bloody battlefield in past ages," preserving the Union and "future glory of this great sanctuary of freedom," the enlistment bounty of $138 and survivors' benefits for those who "fall at the post of duty." Nowhere was a desire to restrict or abolish slavery mentioned.

The expansion of war aims announced in the Preliminary Emancipation Proclamation (see Chapter 8) brought new challenges to Boston's Irish community. In October 1862, *The Pilot* expressed its fervent hope that the pending midterm elections would result in a sufficiently Democratic Congress such that Lincoln would reconsider issuing the promised Emancipation Proclamation. The paper also suggested that even if offered freedom, the vast majority of slaves would reject it because the "servile plantation is the life intended for them." When Lincoln did issue the Emancipation Proclamation on January 1, 1863, *The Pilot* accused him of waging an

Recruitment poster for Ninth Regiment Massachusetts Volunteer Infantry. *Courtesy of the Massachusetts Historical Society.*

abolitionist war unsupported by the principles of the Constitution. Slavery opponent Lieutenant Colonel Guiney reported that he could find very few Irishmen "whose views are congenial to me."[76]

Many Irish soldiers also did not welcome blacks into the ranks. Peter Welsh reported that his comrades would not welcome black regiments, as blacks "are looked upon as the principal cause of this war and this feeling is especially strong in the Irish regiments."[77] Blaming the English for inciting "agitation of the slavery question," Welsh emphasized his commitment to supporting the Union in "the first test of a modern free government…against internal enemies and matured rebellion."[78]

This shift in war aims coupled with the continuing high losses sustained by Irish regiments considerably diminished Irish support for the war. After the Union defeat at Chancellorsville in May 1863, *The Pilot* lamented:

> *The Irish spirit for the war is dead! Absolutely dead! There are a great many Irish yet. But our fighters are dead—dead at Manassas, dead at Malvern Hill, dead in the trenches of the Peninsula, dead at Fredericksburg, dead at Chancellorsville—dead in many other fields. It is a fact that our men have been exterminated in this war. Their desperate valor led them not to victory, but to extinction.*

Draft Riots

The length of the war and its mounting death toll left the North concerned about manpower shortages in the army. In March 1863, President Lincoln signed the Enrollment Act, which mandated the registration of all males between the ages of twenty and forty-five, including immigrants who had filed for citizenship. Exemptions from the draft could be bought for $300 or by hiring a substitute. Each state was assigned a quota of new troops to be furnished. Many in the Irish community pledged resistance to the draft; a particular focus of their resentment was the ability of the wealthy to pay for an exemption or to hire a substitute. Not coincidentally, many hired substitutes were impoverished Irishmen.

In Boston, the first conscription notices were delivered on July 14, 1863. Informed by news from New York of Irish-led riots that resulted in death and destruction over the course of four days, Governor Andrew and Boston mayor Frederick Lincoln[79] prepared for possible violence. Troops guarding

Confederate prisoners of war on Georges Island in Boston Harbor and companies of soldiers training in and around Boston were ordered to assist. The soldiers secured a North End armory where a mostly Irish mob of five hundred to one thousand men and women armed with bricks, bats and stones had gathered. As rioters nearly succeeded in breaking down the armory door, the soldiers fired a cannon into the crowd, which then rapidly dispersed. "Several persons were killed and more wounded…how many, probably, will never be known as they were carried away by friends and kept hidden," reported William Schouler, the state's adjutant general.[80] The draft riot came to a quick end.

Several factors may explain the relative brevity of Boston's draft riot as compared to other Northern cities, such as New York and Philadelphia. In those cities, rioters turned their wrath on the black community. Boston had, by comparison, a small black population that had grown little during the war years. Moreover, *The Pilot* and Catholic clergy condemned the riots and emphasized that "[t]here should be no leniency shown to those who take the law into their own hands." Soldier Peter Welsh agreed, writing that every instigator of those riots should be "hung like dogs."[81] In the end, the Enrollment Act had little effect on Boston's Irish population. Many of those called failed to report, and others claimed an exemption based on physical condition or family circumstances. It is likely that less than 1 percent of those served with conscription notices in Boston served.[82]

During the presidential election of 1864, Boston's Irish strongly supported General George McClellan, the Democratic Party nominee, over President Lincoln. In addition to his party affiliation, many Irish felt genuine affection for McClellan. He had won the loyalty of Irish troops by his relentless focus on training and refusal to act in what he considered a precipitous manner, and the Irish community had been dismayed when Lincoln removed him from command in November 1862. *The Pilot* pronounced McClellan the candidate of "the Union under the Constitution," while it accused Lincoln of promising only the continuation of war until it led to "beggary, ruin, and national death."[83] *The Pilot* also praised the Democratic Party's long-standing commitment to the Irish and continued to link the Republican Party to the hated Know Nothings. Irishmen voted overwhelmingly for McClellan.[84]

Though Lincoln's reelection was a disappointment to the Irish, subsequent Union victories meant that the end of the war was finally in sight. Boston's Irish community joined the rest of the city in celebrating the end of war and the triumph of the Union. When Richmond surrendered in April 1865, *The Pilot* rejoiced in "the unconquerable strength in a government of the people whose basis is general intelligence and freedom of conscience and of speech." Days later, after Lincoln's assassination, many Irish joined in grieving his death and eulogized him as a man who, despite his failings, gave himself to the great work of "the salvation of his country."

Following the war, the Irish community in Boston began a long period of economic and political ascension. While the Republicans continued to dominate state politics for many decades, the Democrats and the Irish soon ruled the city itself. Boston elected its first Irish mayor, Hugh O'Brien, in 1884. Boston's third Irish mayor (1906–08), John Francis "Honey Fitz" Fitzgerald, was the grandfather of President John Fitzgerald Kennedy.

Chapter 8

EMANCIPATION!

When the war began in April 1861, the path from slavery to freedom was far from clear. Like President Lincoln, the majority of Northerners believed the purpose of the war was to preserve the Union. They would tolerate slavery in the Southern slave states if those states would rejoin the fold and abandon efforts to expand slavery's footprint. Boston's abolitionists had come around to supporting the Union amid the initial burst of patriotic fervor. Now these activists had a new challenge: to persuade Lincoln and the general public that slavery was the cause of the conflict and that its eradication was therefore essential to both victory and the elimination of any future sectional war.

Boston's abolitionists formed a league to advocate for emancipation. They knew they were in a race against time. A quick Northern victory would leave slavery intact in the Confederate and border states. Unintentionally, the South came to the abolitionists' aid. Confederate military victories early in the war assured prolonged strife and, over time, led the North to recognize the practical need both to deprive the South of its slave labor and to enlist black soldiers (see Chapter 9).

Reflecting their heightened public stature now that war had begun, even radical abolitionists like Garrison and Phillips were welcomed as speakers by antislavery groups throughout the North. Civil War historian James McPherson explains, "When the Union broke apart and war erupted, many persons began to regard the abolitionists in a new light. They no longer appeared as zealous crackpots, but as prophets who had tried to save their country before it was too late."[85]

To attract a broader audience, Garrison and Phillips moderated their most provocative claims. They now explained that their strident calls for disunion had been only a tactic when the North was set on placating Southern slaveholders. Calling for disunion had been a "direct and efficient way of educating the public to a stern antislavery principle," said Phillips. "It leavened their minds and wakened their conscience." Garrison clarified that Southern secession fundamentally differed from the disunion he had formerly championed. Secession was an attempt to deny the legitimacy of the federal government and lawful election results; in contrast, disunion was sanctioned by the right to revolt against injustice set forth in the Declaration of Independence. By the end of 1861, Garrison had changed *The Liberator*'s banner. He removed from the front page his accusation that the Constitution was a covenant with death and now showcased the biblical commandment "Proclaim Liberty throughout the land, to all its inhabitants thereof."

Employing the same strategies that had been so successful decades earlier, the abolitionists wrote pamphlets, lectured and organized petition drives. They strove to create a "great Northern sentiment" against slavery and to persuade audiences that the restoration of the old Union—one with slavery—was "well-nigh impossible." An early focus of the petition drives was the abolition of slavery within Washington, D.C., as Congress unquestionably had authority for such a measure—one that would have both practical and symbolic significance.

As in the antebellum years, the intransigence of Southern leaders inadvertently assisted the abolitionists' efforts. Shortly before war began, Alexander Hamilton Stephens, the vice president of the Confederacy, delivered a speech in Savannah, Georgia (remembered as the "Cornerstone Speech") that unmistakably stated the Southern view of the cause of war:

> [The Confederacy's] *foundations are laid, its cornerstone rests, upon the great truth that the negro is not equal to the white man; that slavery, subordination to the superior race, is his natural and moral condition. This, our new Government, is the first, in the history of the world, based upon this great physical, philosophical, and moral truth.*

In response, Garrison agreed that slavery was the cause of the nation's troubles and divisions, adding, "[T]he removal of it, therefore, is essential to our national existence. What can be plainer than this?" Senator Charles Sumner echoed this emphasis on the inextricable link between war and slavery. He announced at the Republican state convention in October 1861, "It is often said that war will make an end of Slavery. This is probable. But it is surer still that the overthrow of Slavery will make an end of the war."

Contraband

The gradual transformation of Northern war aims began with the act of a former Massachusetts politician. Benjamin Butler was a Democratic lawyer and legislator from the textile city of Lowell. A "cotton Whig," Butler had supported the Compromise of 1850, run as the unsuccessful Democratic nominee for governor in 1859 and campaigned against Lincoln's election in 1860. But he was also a Unionist, and when the war began, he used his extensive political connections to obtain an officer's commission despite having no military experience beyond leading a state militia regiment. On May 16, 1861, Butler was appointed a major general and ordered to secure Fort Monroe. Located on the tip of a peninsula in the Chesapeake Bay, Fort Monroe was a small island of Union blue in a sea of Confederate gray.

Within days of Butler's assuming command, three slaves escaped from a nearby site where Confederate slave owners had ordered them to build fortifications. The Confederate commander visited Butler to demand the slaves' return under the Fugitive Slave Act. Butler refused, stating that "the Fugitive Slave Act did not affect a foreign country, which Virginia claims to be…I shall hold these Negroes as contraband of war, since they are engaged in the construction of your battery and are claimed as your property."

While Butler's rationale was not based on the immorality of slavery, it was nonetheless significant. Regarding fleeing slaves as "contraband" gave Union commanders and soldiers a pragmatic reason for skirting and then undermining the laws protecting slavery. Abolitionists recognized the import of his action. Sumner praised Butler as a "brave general" who "though commencing his career with prejudices derived from the proslavery school of politicians has known how to see this question in its true light."

In Washington, the results of the election of 1860 coupled with Southern secession had left both the House of Representatives and the Senate dominated by Republicans. Congress endorsed Butler's strategy by enacting an Act to Confiscate Property Used for Insurrectionary Purposes (the first Confiscation Act), which authorized unspecified court proceedings to confiscate any property, including slaves, used to support Confederate war efforts. After lobbying by Sumner and other Republican senators, Lincoln signed the legislation. Over time, hundreds and then thousands of slaves sought refuge in Union army camps, bringing the army a helpful source of laborers. At the same time, the new arrivals showed many soldiers from all-white towns the diligent work of black people and their passionate desire for freedom.

Boston's abolitionists were, however, quickly reminded that Lincoln was not yet prepared to take a more radical step. In July 1861, Lincoln appointed John Fremont, the 1856 Republican presidential candidate, commander of the Department of the West and tasked him with preventing the secession of the critical border state of Missouri. Acting without permission from—or even notice to—Lincoln, Fremont issued a decree stating, "The property of any person taking up arms against the United States" is "declared to be confiscated," and their slaves "are hereby declared to be freemen." Fremont's order of emancipation alarmed Lincoln. He feared it might lead Missouri to secede and knew it would anger the many Northerners who remained hostile—or at best indifferent—to the antislavery cause. Lincoln ordered Fremont to revoke his decree. When he refused, Lincoln removed him from command in November 1861. Boston's abolitionists reacted with anger and disgust, with Garrison complaining, "Lincoln might be six feet, four inches tall…but he is only a dwarf in mind."[86]

Fort Warren and the *Trent* Affair

Boston's abolitionists smarting over Fremont's firing soon had a reason to celebrate: secessionists, including two Confederate envoys, were imprisoned in Boston Harbor. Starting in the seventeenth century, Bostonians had

Below: Interior of Fort Warren. *Courtesy of the Boston Pubic Library.*

constructed fortifications on harbor islands to protect their city from possible attack. Fort Warren, named for Dr. Joseph Warren, a Revolutionary War Patriot killed at the Battle of Bunker Hill, was an imposing granite fort located on Georges Island, seven miles off the coast. Initially used as a training camp for Union soldiers, the war department converted Fort Warren to a Union prison in the fall of 1861. Early captives included pro-Confederate members of the Maryland legislature whom President Lincoln had arrested to ensure that the slave state of Maryland would not vote to secede. In November 1861, Confederate diplomats James Mason and John Slidell were also imprisoned there.

A key Confederate strategy was to seek support and, ultimately, recognition from Great Britain, which relied on Southern cotton to power its industrial revolution. Preventing European support for the Confederate nation, by contrast, was vital to the Union. On November 8, 1861, the Confederacy dispatched Mason and Slidell, both former U.S. senators, to Britain and France to lobby for aid and recognition. Part of their scheduled journey was aboard a British mail ship, the *Trent*. Union captain Charles Wilkes, commanding the USS *Jacinto*, encountered the *Trent* near the coast of Cuba and seized Mason and Slidell.

The Northern public celebrated this news, which softened the blow of the recent routs of Union forces at Bull Run and Ball's Bluff. Captain Wilkes was lionized as a new hero by Boston's abolitionists. However, a crisis ensued when Britain learned of the seizure. Angrily asserting that the United States had violated international law by seizing and boarding the ship of a neutral party in international waters, Britain threatened war unless the diplomats were released with an official apology.

While governments debated their fates, Mason and Slidell resided in officers' quarters at Fort Warren. Mason wrote to his wife on November 29, 1861: "[We] have two rooms and a closet attached, good beds; and are allowed to get from Boston anything we want, and also have a good servant. We mess [eat] with the Maryland prisoners and officers of the army and navy confined here…we have a better daily table than any hotel affords."

By late December, Lincoln was convinced that avoiding war with Britain required his releasing Slidell and Mason. Sumner, now serving as chair of the Senate Foreign Relations Committee, was instrumental in achieving a face-saving but effective resolution. The Lincoln administration would concede that the seizure violated international law but assert—truthfully—that Wilkes had acted without orders. Sumner's support convinced abolitionists that the envoys had to be released. Slidell and Mason were set free on New Year's

Day 1862 and continued their journey. Despite the economic advantages to Britain, their mission was a difficult one. Britain had abolished slavery throughout its territories back in 1833. As for Lincoln, he realized that until the North included ending slavery as a war aim, the door was open to a British-Confederate alliance.

"Battle Hymn of the Republic"

Following the release of Slidell and Mason, abolitionists intensified their campaign for emancipation. They argued that European powers would not consider an alliance with the Confederacy if the North were committed to ending slavery. Garrison also stressed to Republicans that the war had erased any meaningful distinction between abolitionists and Free Soilers, as all within the antislavery community shared a commitment to a free government and the principles of the Declaration of Independence. Emancipation, he argued, should not be controversial. It would "destroy nothing but evil…it [would] make freedom and education and invention and enterprise and prosperity and peace and a true Union possible and sure."

The abolitionists' efforts were bolstered when Julia Ward Howe's abolitionist poem "Battle Hymn of the Republic" was published in the *Atlantic Monthly* in February 1862. Howe, a Bostonian, was the wife of Samuel Gridley Howe, one of the "Secret Six" who had financed John Brown's raid at Harpers Ferry.

The story of this famous song also stems from Fort Warren, but while it still served as a Union army training camp early in the war. While stationed there, members of the Second Infantry Battalion of the Massachusetts Militia created the verses of the poem "John Brown's Body" and set it to the tune of a well-

Julia Ward Howe. *Courtesy of the Library of Congress.*

THE ATLANTIC MONTHLY.

A MAGAZINE OF LITERATURE, ART, AND POLITICS.

VOL. IX.—FEBRUARY, 1862.—NO. LII.

BATTLE HYMN OF THE REPUBLIC.

MINE eyes have seen the glory of the coming of the Lord:
He is trampling out the vintage where the grapes of wrath are stored;
He hath loosed the fateful lightning of His terrible swift sword:
        His truth is marching on.

I have seen Him in the watch-fires of a hundred circling camps,
They have builded Him an altar in the evening dews and damps;
I can read His righteous sentence by the dim and flaring lamps:
        His day is marching on.

I have read a fiery gospel writ in burnished rows of steel:
"As ye deal with my contemners, so with you my grace shall deal;
Let the Hero, born of woman, crush the serpent with his heel,
        Since God is marching on."

He has sounded forth the trumpet that shall never call retreat;
He is sifting out the hearts of men before His judgment-seat:
Oh, be swift, my soul, to answer Him! be jubilant, my feet!
        Our God is marching on.

In the beauty of the lilies Christ was born across the sea,
With a glory in his bosom that transfigures you and me:
As he died to make men holy, let us die to make men free,
        While God is marching on.

"Battle Hymn of the Republic" as it appeared in the *Atlantic Monthly* in February 1862. *Courtesy of the Atlantic Monthly Group.*

known hymn. Their creative inspiration was sparked by the coincidence that a battalion member, a Scottish immigrant, shared the militant abolitionist's name. "John Brown's Body" quickly spread and became popular among Union soldiers.

Howe was inspired to write grander lyrics to the tune of "John Brown's Body" in November 1861 after she attended a review of Union troops in Washington, D.C. The words came to her one memorable night:

> *I went to bed and slept as usual, but awoke the next morning in the gray of the early dawn, and to my astonishment found that the wished-for lines were arranging themselves in my brain. I lay quite still until the last verse had completed itself in my thoughts, then hastily arose, saying to myself, "I shall lose this if I don't write it down immediately." I searched for an old sheet of paper and an old stub of a pen which I had had the night before, and began to scrawl the lines almost without looking.*[87]

"Battle Hymn of the Republic" became instantly popular. In several simple stanzas, it repositioned the war as a moral and religious crusade in which Northerners were divinely inspired to purge the nation of the sin of slavery.[88]

> *He has sounded forth the trumpet that shall never call retreat;*
> *He is sifting out the hearts of men before His judgment-seat:*
> *In the beauty of the lilies Christ was born across the sea,*
> *With a glory in His bosom that transfigures you and me.*
> *As He died to make men holy, let us die to make men free,*
> *While God is marching on.*

Howe's lyrics left no room for ambiguity about the causes and costs of the war—the suffering and dying was in pursuit of a higher cause. When Lincoln first heard it, he was reportedly moved to tears.

The Preliminary Emancipation Proclamation

Significant congressional action followed during the spring of 1862. Congress acted to end slavery in the District of Columbia, prohibit slavery in all U.S. territories and forbid army and navy officers from returning fugitive slaves. In March 1862, Wendell Phillips traveled to Washington, where he was accorded the honor of a private meeting with Lincoln. Phillips left the meeting "rather encouraged" that the president was moving in the right direction. Several months later, Congress passed the Second Confiscation and Militia Act, which held that all slaves of persons "engaged in rebellion against the government of the United States" shall be "forever free of their servitude and not again held as slaves." That law also authorized Lincoln to enlist blacks into the U.S. Army, although he limited them to working as low-paid laborers.

Despite signing this law on July 17, 1862, Lincoln doubted its legality. He felt more confident of his own presidential wartime authority (as commander in chief) to issue a limited emancipation plan if it was justified by military necessity.

Boston's abolitionists had played a key role in persuading the president of his wartime authority to free slaves. As early as the 1840s, congressman and former president John Quincy Adams had argued that if the slaveholding states were to engage in war, the president's constitutional authority could legally extend to ordering the "universal emancipation of the slaves." Attorney David Lee Child, the spouse of abolitionist Lydia Maria Child, published a pamphlet in 1861 making a persuasive legal case that the doctrine of military necessity provided ample wartime authority for an executive order of emancipation.

By the summer of 1862, Lincoln had concluded that emancipation was a necessary tactical weapon toward restoration of the Union. Emancipation would deprive the Confederacy of slave labor and make black manpower available to the Union army. It would remove the threat of European support for the Confederacy. On July 22, 1862, Lincoln shared with his cabinet a draft of a proposed Preliminary Emancipation Proclamation. It provided for freeing all slaves in areas still in rebellion on January 1, 1863.

Lincoln delayed issuing the proclamation on the advice of Secretary of State William Seward. He counseled Lincoln to issue it only after a military victory as, otherwise "it may be viewed as the last measure of an exhausted government, a cry for help…our last shriek on the retreat."[89]

Unaware that Lincoln planned to issue the Preliminary Emancipation Proclamation, abolitionists spent the summer of 1862 fretting about Lincoln's commitment to the antislavery cause. Their fears were fueled when he masked his intent in a letter to influential *New York Tribune* editor Horace Greeley on August 22, 1862. Lincoln wrote:

> *My paramount object in this struggle is to save the Union, and is not either to save or to destroy slavery. If I could save the Union without freeing any slave I would do it, and if I could save it by freeing all the slaves I would do it; and if I could save it by freeing some and leaving others alone I would also do that. What I do about slavery, and the colored race, I do because I believe it helps to save the Union; and what I forbear, I forbear because I do not believe it would help to save the Union.*

By late summer, worries hung in Boston's muggy air. Garrison's wife wrote, "We are feeling extremely anxious about the country. We have come to the conclusion that Lincoln will not declare emancipation."[90] One Massachusetts abolitionist wrote of attending a war rally where "there was not much to stir the soul" and the compelling need for "some great eternal principle to make our Country seem worth fighting for."[91] Lydia Maria Child sought to reach Lincoln directly. She wrote a public letter to him in which she acknowledged the "extreme difficulties of his position" but criticized his excessive trust in selfish diplomats and politicians and his seeming lack of confidence in the "the people." "Are you not aware that moral enthusiasm is the mightiest of all forces?" she asked. "I beseech you not to check the popular enthusiasm for freedom! Would that you could realize what a mighty power there is in the heart of a free people."

Lincoln continued not to tip his hand, but waited for a propitious moment to announce his decree. The Battle of Antietam, on September 17, 1862, finally provided an opportunity. During that bloodiest day in United States history, the Union army repelled General Lee's invasion of Maryland. Claiming Antietam as a decisive Union victory,[92] Lincoln issued the Preliminary Emancipation Proclamation five days later. He promised:

> *That on the first day of January in the year of our Lord, one thousand eight hundred and sixty-three, all persons held as slaves within any State, or designated part of a State, the people whereof shall then be in rebellion against the United States shall be then, thenceforward, and forever free; and the executive government of the United States, including the military and naval authority thereof, will recognize and maintain the freedom of such persons, and will do no act or acts to repress such persons, or any of them, in any efforts they may make for their actual freedom.*

The decree exempted the border states as well as areas under Union army control, called for continued efforts at colonization and postponed its effective date for one hundred days. The limited reach of the proclamation drew both praise and condemnation from abolitionists. But criticism was generally muted, as abolitionists understood that the Emancipation Proclamation, even if limited and qualified, would transform the goals of the war. Governor Andrew wrote, "It is a poor document, but a mighty act; slow, somewhat halting, wrong in its delay until January, but grand and sublime after all."[93]

The tension-filled one hundred days before January 1 included both congressional and state elections. Democrats accused Lincoln of mismanaging the military effort and of wrongly injecting the issue of emancipation into a war to restore the Union. The election results revealed that the nation as a whole did not entirely support the new war aims: Democrats gained more than thirty seats in the House of Representatives. However, in Massachusetts, the Republicans gained strength as more people recognized that emancipation was a necessary prerequisite to the restoration of a stable Union.

The Massachusetts legislature voted overwhelmingly to return Charles Sumner to the Senate. Governor Andrew was also reelected, defeating Charles Devens, the U.S. marshal who had orchestrated Thomas Sims's return to slavery in 1851. Republican Frederic Lincoln defeated Boston mayor Joseph Wightman, who had cautioned President Lincoln several months earlier that the Hub's abolitionists were not representative of the city's residents.[94]

THE EMANCIPATION PROCLAMATION

New Year's Day 1863 dawned with great anticipation—and nagging fears. Would Lincoln sign the Emancipation Proclamation as promised, or would the Republican losses in the midterm elections induce him to back down? Had he offered the slaveholders yet another chance for reconciliation? Abolitionists had greeted with dismay Lincoln's December 1, 1862 message to Congress, in which he laid out plans for both gradual, compensated emancipation and colonization of emancipated slaves in Haiti and Liberia. In mid-December, Harriet Beecher Stowe wrote to Senator Sumner, "Everybody I meet in New England says to me with anxious earnestness—'Will the President stand firm to his Proclamation?'"[95] Frederick Douglass later recalled worries that Lincoln's "boundless patience" would lead to yet another effort at "peace and reconciliation."

Hub of the Second Revolution

Crowds of excited, anxious Bostonians gathered at both the Tremont Temple Baptist Church and Boston's Music Hall, located a block apart, to await the news. At Tremont Temple, the mostly black crowd of three thousand heard from speakers including Frederick Douglass, William Cooper Nell and John Rock. Nell, who presided over the meeting, announced that soon, "from the Atlantic to the Pacific, there shall not be found a tyrant to wield the lash, nor a slave to wear the chain." But impatient with Lincoln's slow pace, Nell called emancipation the policy of Fremont and Sumner.[96]

Henry Wadsworth Longfellow, Ralph Waldo Emerson and Oliver Wendell Holmes Sr. were among the organizers of a Grand Jubilee Concert at the Music Hall, attended by a mostly white crowd. The program booklet confidently predicted that January 1, 1863, would "prove the complement of the 4th of July, 1776." Emerson prepared his "Boston Hymn" for the occasion. One stanza follows:

I break your bonds and masterships,
And I unchain the slave:
Free be his heart and hand henceforth,
As wind and wandering wave.

As the day went on with no news from those waiting at a nearby telegraph office, members of both Boston audiences became increasingly tense. They were unaware that Lincoln had delayed signing the Emancipation Proclamation until after the White House New Year's reception so that a technical error in the initial version could be fixed. A further delay came about because Lincoln's hand was trembling from shaking hundreds of hands at the afternoon reception. He postponed the signing until he was sure he could affix a signature as firm as his conviction. Not until evening did word arrive that

Ralph Waldo Emerson. *Courtesy of the Library of Congress.*

President Abraham Lincoln in 1863 by Alexander Gardner. *Courtesy of the Library of Congress.*

Lincoln had signed the Emancipation Proclamation and that the text would soon be transmitted. The crowds erupted into joyous celebration.

The Emancipation Proclamation was narrowly crafted. It ended slavery only in those states, or portions of states, under rebellion, thus leaving slavery intact in the border states and areas under Union army control. But it cast a broader sweep than the preliminary proclamation in several important respects. It provided for those formerly enslaved to join the Union army (see Chapter 9) and injected a moral tone into the proclamation, which described itself as an "act of justice." Significantly, this time, the issues of colonization, gradualism and compensation to slaveholders were left out.

Boston's abolitionists recognized that the Proclamation, no matter its limits, sounded the death knell of slavery. Garrison wrote in *The Liberator* that it was "sublime in its magnitude, momentous and beneficent in its far-reaching consequences…" Of the antislavery movement, he proclaimed, "[T]hirty years ago we were in the arctic regions, surrounded by icebergs; today we are in the tropics, with the flowers blooming and the birds singing around us."

Nell remarked that New Year's Day would be "henceforth invested with new significance and imperishable glory in the calendar of time." Douglass "saw in its spirit a life and power far beyond its letter…[The war] was no longer a mere strife for territory and dominion, but a contest of civilization against barbarism." Charles Sumner exalted, "On that day, an angel appeared upon the earth." Maria Weston Chapman was reportedly too overcome with emotion to do more that utter a series of joyous exclamations. In a speech several days later at the Music Hall, Phillips agreed that the Proclamation had "launched" the nation into a "new channel."[97]

The Emancipation Proclamation was a major step in the nation's second revolution. Three decades after the abolitionist movement had dedicated itself to disproving Daniel Webster's slave-tolerant coda, his words were repurposed as a new aim for the nation: "Liberty and Union, now and forever, one and inseparable."

Chapter 9

BLACK SOLDIERS AND CITIZENS

On May 28, 1863, nearly five months after Lincoln issued the Emancipation Proclamation, joyful crowds lined Boston's streets to watch a parade. Marching in step were the newly trained privates of the Fifty-fourth Regiment Massachusetts Volunteer Infantry, the Union army's first black regiment recruited from the North.[98] As the soldiers traced the path Anthony Burns and Thomas Sims had taken when they were forcibly returned to slavery, participants and spectators were acutely aware of the event's historical significance.

Black men had longed to fight for the Union since war appeared on the horizon. Although blacks had fought for the nation in both the American Revolution and the War of 1812, the Lincoln administration at first was determined to have an all-white army subdue the Southern "rebellion."[99] To include black soldiers risked losing the support of those many Northerners who opposed freeing slaves as a war aim. Boston's black activists and radical white abolitionists were just as resolved that black soldiers would join the U.S. Army. Their war was, after all, against both slavery and racism.

Leaders of Boston's black community had begun to lay the groundwork for black soldiers years earlier. In 1855, Robert Morris led an unsuccessful petition effort seeking permission to organize a black state militia unit. Undeterred, black leaders formed the all-black Massasoit Guard—named after a Wampanoag chief who befriended the Pilgrims at Plymouth—without state support. When the war began, John Rock and Lewis Hayden organized the Home Guard, a drill company of black men, and offered their services in the war effort.[100] Twenty-nine black men in Boston renewed their efforts to ask the state legislature to remove the word "white" from the state militia law, writing in a petition:

> *We make this prayer first because such a distinction is anomalous to the spirit of justice and equality pervading all the other laws of this commonwealth. Secondly because we desire to be recognized by the law as competent to and worthy of defending our homes and the government that protects those homes.*[101]

The Massachusetts legislature did not respond. The Federal Militia Act, which limited eligibility to white men, governed the recruitment of Union forces, and legislators were in addition unwilling to risk rending the state's newfound unity.

When Secretary of War Simon Cameron declared that he had no intention of calling black soldiers to serve in the army, Frederick Douglass denounced this injustice:

> *Our Presidents, Governors, Generals and Secretaries are calling, with almost frantic vehemence, for men. "Men! men! Send us men!" they scream, or the cause of the Union is gone…and yet these very officers, representing the people and the Government, steadily and persistently refuse to receive the very class of men which have a deeper interest in the defeat and humiliation of the rebels than all others.*

Radical white abolitionists echoed his plea. Governor Andrew said in 1861, "When any man comes to the standard and desires to defend the flag, [we will not] find it important to light a candle to see what is the complexion of his face, or to consult the family Bible to ascertain whether his grandfather came from the banks of the Thames or the banks of the Senegal."[102] Some credit Lewis Hayden, who had a close relationship with Andrew, with persuading the governor to take a public stance on this divisive subject so early in the war. During the next sixteen months, Andrew and Boston's black leaders would continuously press the issue of black military service.

The Union would reconsider its policy in 1862 when military leaders sought the additional manpower that black soldiers could provide. An army leader again took matters into his own hands. Following his capture of Fort Pulaski near Savannah, Georgia, Colonel David Hunter began to enlist black soldiers from the districts he occupied. Lincoln curtly ordered him to halt, stating, "No commanding general shall do such a thing…without consulting me." But many Republicans supported Hunter's recruitment, and Congress subsequently provided in the Second Confiscation and Militia Act of 1862 that blacks could serve "for the purpose of constructing entrenchments or performing camp service work as military laborers."

Unlike its preliminary predecessor, the Emancipation Proclamation permitted freed slaves to join the armed forces "to garrison forts, positions, stations, and other places, and to man vessels of all sorts in said service." Charles Sumner and Boston merchant George Livermore are widely credited with shifting Lincoln's thinking on this topic during the one hundred days following the Preliminary Emancipation Proclamation. Sumner sent Lincoln a copy of Livermore's newly penned *Historical Research Respecting the Opinions of the Founders of the Republic on Negroes as Slaves and Citizens and as Soldiers*.

Although the Emancipation Proclamation did not explicitly mention freemen, Governor Andrew immediately sought permission to raise a black regiment in Massachusetts. Secretary of War Edwin Stanton agreed and issued the following order on January 26, 1863: "Governor Andrew of Massachusetts is authorized, until further orders, to raise such number of volunteer companies…such volunteers to be enlisted for three years or until sooner discharged, and may include persons of African descent, organized into separate corps." To placate the many Northerners who objected to black soldiers and doubted the competency of black officers, Stanton stipulated that white officers had to lead the newly formed black regiments.

THE FIFTY-FOURTH REGIMENT

Though disappointed by the prohibition on black officers, Andrew sought out white men of abolitionist sympathies and exemplary skills and morals to lead the regiment. For regimental colonel, Andrew had his eye on twenty-six-year-old Robert Gould Shaw, the son of committed abolitionists Francis and Sarah Shaw. Robert, who had attended Harvard, initially enlisted in the Seventh New York National Guard. He was then commissioned as a lieutenant in the Second Regiment Massachusetts Volunteer Infantry, where he fought in several battles, including Antietam, and was promoted to captain. Seeking to persuade Robert to agree to accept command of this new regiment, Governor Andrew wrote to Robert's father and asked him to persuade his son to accept command:

I am about to raise a Colored Regiment in Massachusetts. This I cannot but regard as perhaps the most important corps to be organized during the whole war...I am desirous to have for its officers—particularly for its field officers—young men of military experience, of firm Anti Slavery principles, ambitions, superior to a vulgar contempt for color, and having faith in the capacity of colored men for military service. Such officers must be necessarily gentlemen of the highest tone and honor...it occurs to me to offer the Colonelcy of such a Regiment to your son, Captain Shaw of the 2nd Mass. Infantry.

Colonel Robert Gould Shaw. *Courtesy of the Library of Congress.*

Francis Shaw personally delivered Governor Andrew's letter to his son. Robert initially thought to decline the invitation. However, he changed his mind the following day and explained to his fiancée, Annie Haggerty, "I feel I should never regret having taken this step, as far as I myself am concerned; for while I was undecided I felt ashamed of myself, as if I were cowardly." Shaw also wrote that many eminent men considered a black regiment of the "greatest importance to our country" and, while hopeful that black soldiers would not meet with as much opposition as first supposed, he "shan't be frightened out of it by its unpopularity; and I hope you won't care if it is made fun of."[103]

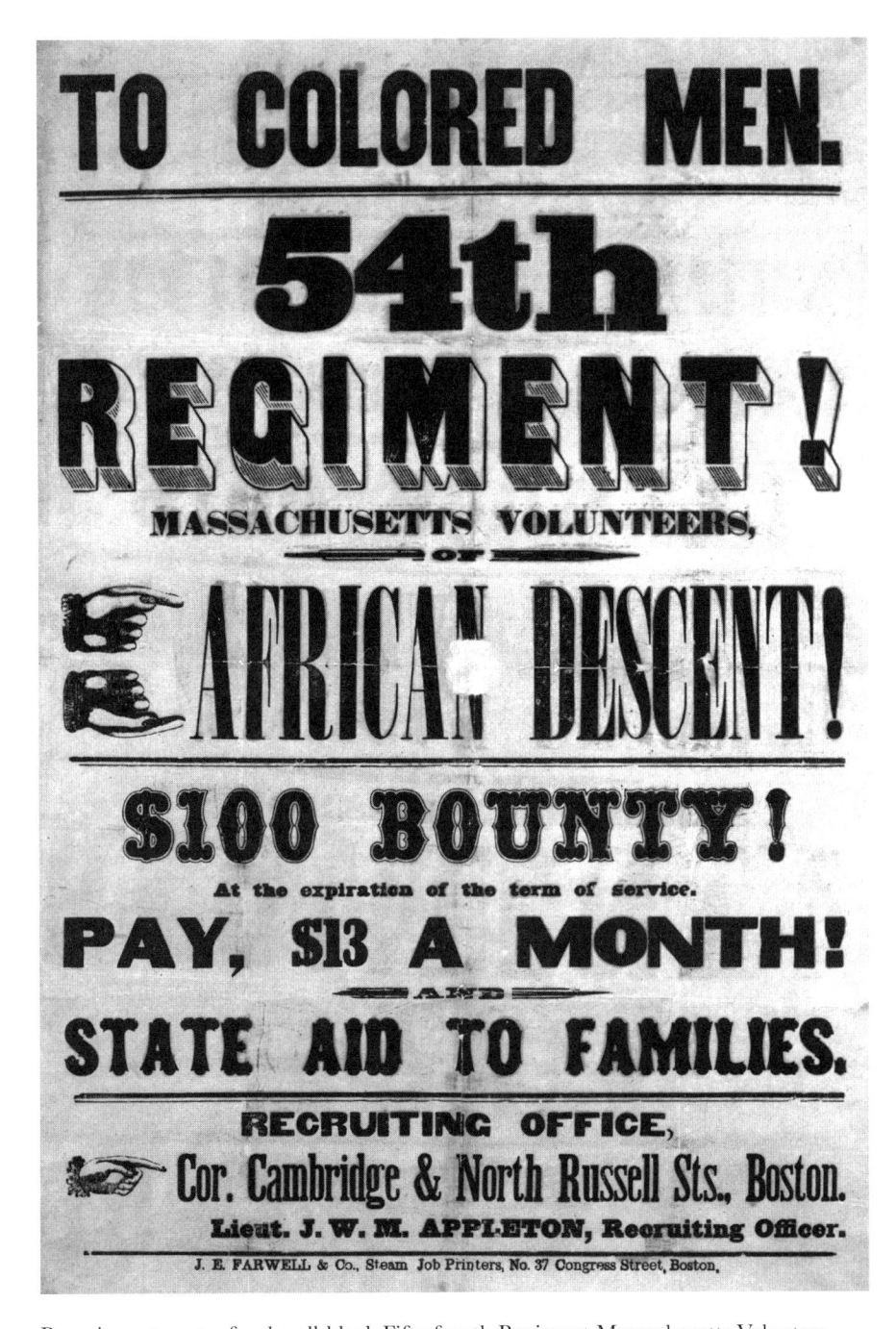

Recruitment poster for the all-black Fifty-fourth Regiment Massachusetts Volunteer Infantry, the first black regiment raised in the North. *Courtesy of the Massachusetts Historical Society.*

Recruitment of the black regiment proceeded slowly at first, as the entire state of Massachusetts had fewer than two thousand men eligible to serve (out of a black population of nine thousand).[104] Moreover, several community leaders, including Rock and Morris, were so irate that white officers would be in command that they advised against enlistment. But other black leaders, including Nell, Hayden and Reverend Leonard Grimes, urged enlistment because they believed that black soldiers would advance the cause of equality. Douglass was an enthusiastic proponent of enlistment. "Never since the world began was there a better chance offered to a long enslaved and oppressed people," he stated. "Once let the black man get upon his person the brass letters U.S., let him get an eagle on his button, and a musket on his shoulder, and bullets in his pocket; and there is no power on the earth, or under the earth, that can deny that he has earned the right of citizenship in the United States." Douglass also reminded blacks of the special status of Massachusetts and its politicians in the struggle for freedom: "She was the first in the War of Independence, first to break the chain of her slaves, first to make the black man equal before the law, first to admit colored children to her common schools, and she was the first to answer with her blood the alarm-cry of the nation when its capital was menaced by rebels."

Two of Douglass's sons, Lewis and Charles, enlisted, and the African Meeting House became a recruitment center. By early May 1863, one thousand men from twenty-two states filled the Fifty-fourth Regiment, and a second regiment, the Fifty-fifth, was formed from the surplus. These new recruits were particularly fit for battle. Seeking to create an exemplary first cadre of black soldiers, Governor Andrew arranged for exceptionally strict physical exams, and nearly one-third of those who volunteered were rejected.[105]

The Fifty-fourth Regiment trained for several months at Camp Meigs in Readville in what is today Boston's Hyde Park neighborhood. James Henry Gooding, a recruit from New Bedford who wrote regular dispatches to the *New Bedford Mercury*, his hometown's abolitionist newspaper, reported in early April: "The 54th progresses daily…these noble men are practically refuting the base assertions…that the black race are incapable of patriotism, valor or ambition."[106]

The Confederacy, meanwhile, reacted to the arming of black soldiers by announcing that, if captured, they would not be treated as prisoners of war. The Confederates pledged that any black captured fighting for the Union would be executed or enslaved and that any white commander of black troops would face a death sentence. Lincoln promised retaliation if the Confederates carried out these threats.

Hub of the Second Revolution

On May 18, Governor Andrew visited Camp Meigs to present the Fifty-fourth Regiment with the United States flag, the Massachusetts state flag and its regimental banners. Reverend Grimes offered a prayer, and Governor Andrew told the new soldiers:

> *Today we recognize the right of every man in this Commonwealth to be a MAN and a citizen. We see before us a band of noble men as ever came together for a great and glorious cause. They go not for themselves alone, but they go to vindicate a foul aspersion that they were not men…We see a great and glorious future spread out before us, when the principles of right and justice shall govern our beloved country.*

On May 28, 1863, the men of the Fifty-fourth Massachusetts Volunteer Infantry paraded in uniform past the twenty thousand Bostonians who lined the city's streets before boarding ships bound for Beaufort, South Carolina. Garrison watched from a nearby balcony, his hand resting on a bust of abolitionist John Brown. Noting the scant number of protesters, Boston flour merchant Samuel Bowdlear concluded, "The prejudice here against employing colored soldiers [is] dying out gradually. The idea seems at last to have got through many thick heads that it is no more than right that the 'darkies' should do their share of the fighting." Augustus St. Gaudens's magnificent statue of Robert Gould Shaw and the Massachusetts Fifty-fourth Regiment Memorial, erected on the Boston Common across from the Massachusetts State House in 1897, recalls this groundbreaking march through the city.[107]

During their first weeks in South Carolina, the regiment formed up within a brigade commanded by Colonel James Montgomery. On June 10, he ordered the Fifty-fourth Regiment, along with the Second South Carolina Volunteers—composed of former slaves—and the Second Rhode Island Battery, to participate in a raid against Darien, Georgia. When the Union soldiers arrived, Darien was a ghost town, for the Confederate soldiers and nearly all of the town's residents had fled in advance of the Union troops. Montgomery ordered the men to seize all property of value and then burn the town. Shaw was horrified but lacked the authority to countermand the order of his senior commander. He described the plunder and burning of Darien in a letter to his wife (he had married on May 2) and asked her not to breathe a word about it since "I have not yet made up my mind what I ought to do. Besides my own distaste for this barbarous sort of warfare, I am not sure it will not harm very much the reputation of black troops and of those

Boston and the Civil War

Six black soldiers of the Fifty-fourth Regiment. *From left to right*: Jeremiah Rolls, first sergeant, Company I; Abram C. Simms, corporal, Company I; George Lipscomb, corporal, Company I; Thomas Bowman, sergeant, Company I; Isom Ampey, private, Company K; and John H. Wilson, sergeant, major. These photos appeared in a regimental history written by Luis F. Emilio, a commander of Company E. *Courtesy of the Boston Pubic Library.*

connected with them."[108] Shaw concluded his letter by wondering whether he should in the future obey orders or refuse and risk arrest and possible court-martial. His life would be cut short without his having to choose.

The Battle of Fort Wagner

The Fifty-fourth Regiment was ordered to James Island, South Carolina, on July 8, 1863, several days after the pivotal Union victory at the Battle of Gettysburg. James Island is one of several small islands in the harbor of Charleston. A week later, nearly one thousand Confederates attacked two hundred soldiers of the Fifty-fourth serving on picket duty. The black soldiers' fierce resistance forced the Confederates to fall back and abandon a planned attack against the Tenth Connecticut Regiment. James Henry Gooding described the reaction of the grateful Connecticut soldiers: "It is not for us to blow our horn; but when a regiment of white men gave us three cheers as we were passing them, it shows that we did our duty as men should."[109] That evening, Shaw wrote to his wife, "What we [the Fifty-fourth] have done today wipes out the remembrance of the Darien affair… the officers and privates of other regiments praise us very much. All this is very gratifying to us personally, and a fine thing for the coloured troops."[110]

The Fifty-fourth Regiment was then ordered to Morris Island, the site of Fort Wagner. Taking the heavily fortified Confederate fort was a vital prerequisite to a successful assault on Fort Sumter and all of Charleston. The city had both a symbolic and strategic significance. Secession had begun in this stronghold of slavery and states' rights. Charleston's harbor and railroad lines made it a crucial transportation and communications center for the South.

On July 18, 1863, the Fifty-fourth Regiment led several thousand Union troops in a ground assault against Fort Wagner. The previous day, Union warships had fired heavy shells at the fort to cripple its defenses. But Union commanders were unaware that the nearly all of the 1,700 Confederate soldiers within had been sheltered by an immense "bombproof, " a fortified shelter with a ceiling protected by nearly ten feet of sand.

To reach the fort, Union troops had to cross open, sandy ground liberally sprinkled with large, water-filled ditches. Shouting "Forward, Fifty-fourth!" Shaw led his men. "Fort Wagner became a mound of fire, from which poured a stream of shot and shell," Captain Luis Emilio later recalled. "Just a brief

Union soldiers, led by the Fifty-fourth Regiment, storm Fort Wagner on Morris Island, South Carolina. *Courtesy of the Library of Congress.*

lull, and the deafening explosions of cannon were renewed, mingled with the crash and rattle of musketry. A sheet of flame, followed by a running fire, like electric sparks, swept along the parapet."[111] The murderous Confederate fusillade killed many troops before they could reach the fort; many others, including Shaw, were killed as they attempted to scale the walls of the fort. The valiant but doomed battle for Fort Wagner forms the centerpiece of the 1989 Academy Award–winning film *Glory*.

By the time Union forces withdrew, their casualties exceeded 1,500. Over 100 men of the Fifty-fourth Massachusetts were killed or captured. Many others were wounded. Lewis Douglass captured the terror and toll of the battle, writing that "men fell all around me. A shell would explode and clear a space of twenty feet. Our men would close up again but it was no use—we had to retreat, which was a very hazardous undertaking."

The Confederates attempted to sully Shaw's memory by burying him in a common trench with his black soldiers. Yet when Shaw's father learned of his son's burial place, he declared, "We can imagine no holier place than that in which he lies, among his brave and devoted followers, nor wish for him better company. What a bodyguard he has."

William Harvey Carney, a former slave who had been promoted to the noncommissioned rank of sergeant, was later awarded the Medal of Honor for his bravery in rescuing the regiment's state flag during the battle.[112] When the flag bearer was shot, Carney took up the flag and led the way to the parapet. When the troops were forced to retreat, he saved the flag despite being severely wounded in the head and leg. As he was brought into the field hospital nearly faint from loss of blood, Carney reportedly announced to his wounded comrades, "Boys, the old flag never touched the ground."

The bravery of the men of the Fifty-fourth at Fort Wagner largely dispelled any concerns that black soldiers would not fight effectively. Lewis Douglass wrote to his fiancée shortly after the battle, "This regiment has established its reputation as a fighting regiment—not a man flinched, though it was a trying time." He added, "I wish we had a hundred thousand colored troops. We would put an end to this war." Others concurred. The *New York Times* was among many Northern newspapers praising the black soldiers. It wrote, "Could any one from the North see these brave fellows as they lie here, their prejudice against them, if he had any, would all pass away."

Sergeant William Harvey Carney with the flag he saved at Fort Wagner. This photo appears in a regimental history written by Luis F. Emilio, a commander of Company E. *Courtesy of the Boston Pubic Library*.

The survivors of the Fifty-fourth Regiment subsequently participated in the lengthy siege of Fort Wagner. After relentless artillery bombardments, the fort finally surrendered to Union forces on September 7, 1863. Despite this success, Charleston was not occupied until February 18, 1865, following a 567-day siege. During the remainder of the war, the Fifty-fourth participated in several additional battles, including the February 1864 Battle of Olustee,

Florida, a bloody Union defeat in which James Henry Gooding, who had been promoted to corporal, was injured and taken prisoner. He died several months later in the notorious Confederate prison of Andersonville, located in Georgia. The Fifty-fourth Regiment subsequently joined General William Tecumseh Sherman's eastward march to the sea.

THE FIFTY-FIFTH REGIMENT AND THE FIFTH CAVALRY

The Fifty-fifth Regiment, formed from the overflow of men who volunteered for the Fifty-fourth, left Boston two months after the Fifty-fourth Regiment—several days after the Battle of Fort Wagner. George Garrison, a son of William Lloyd Garrison, was among its white officers. The regiment arrived in Charleston Harbor in early August 1863 and participated in the successful siege of Fort Wagner. The Fifty-fifth Regiment was also sent to Florida (although not used in battle there) and later fought in the Battle of Honey Hill in South Carolina on November 30, 1864. This battle occurred when Confederate forces stopped Union soldiers attempting to sever tracks of the Charleston & Savannah Railroad in advance of General Sherman's forces. One of the soldiers who participated described the conditions the regiment faced with bravery: "It was like rushing into the very mouth of death…The order [to advance] was promptly obeyed and we rushed in cheering and yelling. But ah! 'twas useless."[113] The Fifty-fifth Regiment suffered 120 casualties.

During the Battle of Honey Hill, Andrew Jackson Smith, a self-emancipated slave who had enlisted in the Fifty-fifth Regiment, retrieved the regimental flags from the fallen color-bearer and carried them back to the Union lines. Though nominated for the Medal of Honor, Smith was not awarded it, as the army claimed that his feat could not be proven due to a lack of official records. Following a reexamination of the historical records, President Bill Clinton posthumously awarded the medal to Smith in 2001, 137 years after the battle.[114]

Governor Andrew capitalized on the positive reports about the Fifty-fourth and Fifty-fifth Regiments' battle exploits by seeking permission to recruit a black cavalry regiment. Secretary of War Stanton consented and also acceded to Andrew's demand that he appoint all of its officers. The Fifth Cavalry was commanded by Henry S. Russell; second in command and later in command was Charles Francis Adams Jr., the son of former Free

Corporal Andrew Jackson Smith of the Fifty-fifth Regiment Massachusetts Volunteer Infantry. *Courtesy of the State Library of Massachusetts.*

Soil Party presidential candidate Charles Francis Adams. The Fifth Cavalry served primarily infantry-dismounted (mostly as prison guards), but the men were mounted during the final weeks of the war.[115]

Near the end of the war, each of the state's three black regiments was among the first to enter key Confederate strongholds. The Fifty-fourth and Fifty-fifth Regiments entered Charleston, South Carolina, following its surrender in February 1865. Wendell Phillips exulted, "Can you conceive a bitterer drop that God's chemistry could mix for the son of the Palmetto State [South Carolina] than that a Massachusetts flag and a colored regiment should take possession of Charleston?" Men of the Fifth Cavalry were among the first to enter the Confederate capital of Richmond, Virginia, when it finally fell on April 3, 1865.

The brave men of these black regiments began a flood that changed the face of the army and helped transform the course of the war. By war's end, 180,000 black men had served in the Union army, comprising approximately 10 percent of Union soldiers. Black soldiers and their abolitionist allies also protested the ban against black officers. At first, the highest rank black soldiers could achieve was that of noncommissioned sergeant. Governor Andrew in 1864 commissioned several black men as second lieutenants, but they did not then receive their commissions from the Union army. However, by the time the war concluded, several men of the Fifty-fourth and Fifty-fifth Regiments had received commissions.

The Battle for Equal Pay

At the same time that black soldiers were proving their capability on the battlefield, they were also engaged in a protracted struggle to be paid the same as their white counterparts. White soldiers were paid $13.00 per month plus a clothing allowance of $3.50. Governor Andrew had received assurance from Secretary of War Stanton that black soldiers would be paid the same amount. However, when the first payday arrived, black soldiers learned that they were to be paid only $7.00 ($10.00 per month in pay with an automatic withdrawal of $3.00 to account for clothing), the same wages as black laborers who worked at jobs such as cooking and ditch digging.

The soldiers refused to accept a laborer's wages and lodged objections. James Henry Gooding appealed directly to President Lincoln, requesting that the men be paid "as American soldiers, not as menial hirelings."[116]

Gooding reminded Lincoln that the worth of the black troops could be found in the many "dusky forms" surrounding Fort Wagner. Members of Company D of the Fifty-fifth Regiment, fully aware that they were fighting against both slavery and racism, succinctly stated, "We came to fight for liberty, justice & equality."[117] Sergeant George E. Stephens wrote of the "unflinching, unswerving loyalty" of black soldiers but cautioned that if the pay disparity was not addressed, "one of the best regiments that ever left Massachusetts will become utterly demoralized."[118]

White commanders, too, pleaded for fair treatment for their men. Six days before he died at Fort Wagner, Colonel Shaw protested that his men should be discharged if not paid equally. After his death, his successor, Lieutenant Colonel Edward N. Hallowell, echoed his plea. Colonel Albert Stedman Hartwell, in command of the Fifty-fifth Regiment, wrote, "I can hardly write, talk, eat or sleep, I am so anxious and indignant that pay is not forthcoming, or official assurance, of pay for my men." Hartwell also noted that "the wives of the men, they say, [are] often reduced to degradation that drives the husbands almost crazy." Governor Andrew also expressed his outrage to President Lincoln, stressing both the soldiers' valor and their families' destitution.

When Congress and the president still did not act, the Massachusetts legislature voted to make up the pay difference. But the soldiers refused to accept this offer for fear of legitimizing the discrimination. They insisted that the duty to rectify the inequity belonged to the U.S. government.

Finally, in June 1864, Congress resolved that black soldiers who were free as of April 19, 1861, would receive the pay promised at the time of enlistment, as well as retroactive pay. Chaplain John R. Bowles of the Fifty-fifth Regiment reported that the men were "in fine spirits and jubilant over the news of the recent victories of the Union army over the rebels, and also the prospect of soon receiving their pay so long withheld."[119] The promised pay did not, however, cover all the soldiers of the all-black Massachusetts regiments, as some had fled from Southern slavery. Commander Hallowell decided to take matters into his own hands. A practicing Quaker, he believed that under God's law, no man was a slave. He composed an oath, known to his men as the "Quaker Oath," which allowed each soldier to claim his status as a free man before April 19, 1861. The uncompromising refusal of these black soldiers to accept unequal pay for military service set an example for future civil rights movements.

Chapter 10

A NEW BIRTH OF FREEDOM

"No such transition of feeling and sentiment, as has taken place within the last four years, stands recorded on the historic page; a change that seems as absolute as it is stupendous," announced William Lloyd Garrison at Boston's Music Hall on February 4, 1865. Abolitionists had gathered to celebrate Congress's adoption of the Thirteenth Amendment to the Constitution. When ratified nine months later, this amendment would permanently abolish slavery in the United States. As Garrison aptly noted, thirty-five years had transformed his reputation from that of a "madman, fanatic, incendiary, [and] traitor" to that of a "true friend of liberty and humanity, animated by the highest patriotism, and devoted to the welfare, peace, unity, and ever increasing prosperity and glory of my native land!" By the end of the year, Garrison would cease publishing *The Liberator*, satisfied that "the object for which [it] was commenced" had been "gloriously consummated."

Work on what would become the Thirteenth Amendment began in 1863, soon after Lincoln promulgated the Emancipation Proclamation. Some abolitionists initially sought a congressional act to buttress Lincoln's wartime decree against potential challenges to its constitutionality. But even a congressional act provided an uncertain bulwark, as a future Congress could rescind it. This was not an idle worry—if the Union prevailed, representatives from the Confederate states would again be part of the national government. Further, slavery proponents would undoubtedly claim that a law banning slavery was unconstitutional given the various endorsements of slavery contained in the Constitution. Sumner and other leading congressional abolitionists therefore proposed a constitutional amendment that would permanently eradicate slavery.

Enacting an amendment would, however, be challenging. Sixty years had passed since the Constitution was last amended. In addition, an amendment would require approval of two-thirds of the members of the House and Senate, followed by ratification by three-quarters of the states. Many Democrats remained opposed to the total, immediate and uncompensated end of slavery or objected to an amendment that could set a precedent for extending the authority of the federal government into the internal affairs of the states.

The Thirteenth Amendment

Buoyed by recent events, the campaign for an amendment began in earnest in December 1863. The Emancipation Proclamation and the recruitment of black soldiers had transformed the strategy and tactics of the war. The Union army's victories at Gettysburg and Vicksburg in July 1863 had improved both its military position and morale. Lincoln's stirring Gettysburg Address, delivered at the November 19, 1863 dedication of the soldiers' cemetery at that battlefield, had memorably recast the basis for war. In only 172 words, Lincoln redefined the nation as one "dedicated to the proposition that all men are created equal" and to the principles of self-government. "We highly resolve that these dead shall not have died in vain—that this nation, under God, shall have a new birth of freedom—and that government of the people, by the people, for the people, shall not perish from the earth."

Lincoln did not, however, offer support for a constitutional amendment in his December 8, 1863 annual message to Congress. He instead promised not "to retract or modify the Emancipation Proclamation" and proposed a Proclamation of Amnesty and Reconstruction that would allow a Confederate state to apply for readmission to the Union when slavery was abolished within it and 10 percent of voters swore allegiance to the Union.

After these forgiving provisions were suggested, some radical abolitionists, including Wendell Phillips, turned against the president. At the January 1864 meeting of the Massachusetts Anti-Slavery Society, Phillips condemned Lincoln for seeking a "sham peace that would betray [the] cause of civil rights." Lincoln's secretaries John F. Nicolay and John Hay later defended

Lincoln's cautious approach. "Prudence was the very essence of Mr. Lincoln's statesmanship, and he doubtless felt it was not safe for the Executive to venture farther at that time," wrote Nicolay and Hay.

Senators and representatives elected by antislavery voters did not feel such constraints, and Republicans introduced amendments to abolish slavery in the House and Senate. Sumner introduced the most radical proposal. He proposed an amendment that would both abolish slavery and guarantee equality before the law: "All persons are equal before the law, so that no person can hold another as a slave; and the Congress shall have power to make all laws necessary and proper to carry this declaration into effect everywhere in the United States."

However, the Senate Judiciary Committee reported out a more limited amendment focused only on the end of slavery.[120] Echoing the language contained in the 1862 act that had ended slavery in national territories, the proposed amendment provided:

> *Section 1. Neither slavery nor involuntary servitude, except as a punishment for crime whereof the party shall have been duly convicted, shall exist within the United States, or any place subject to their jurisdiction.*
> *Section 2. Congress shall have power to enforce this article by appropriate legislation.*

Lucy Stone, Susan B. Anthony and other leading women activists initiated a petition campaign to support congressional passage of the proposed Thirteenth Amendment. In 1863, they had formed the Women's Loyal National League to organize petition drives calling for the immediate end of slavery. The first 100,000 signatures on league petitions were rolled into an enormous bundle and dramatically delivered to Sumner's Senate desk. Petitions containing several hundred thousand additional signatures would soon follow.

Obtaining the necessary two-thirds majority in the Senate was likely, as thirty-six of its fifty members were Republicans. Sumner addressed the Senate on April 8, 1864, shortly before it voted on the amendment. Announcing that it was time for "emancipation of the Constitution itself," he argued that the proposed amendment would "give completeness and permanence to emancipation and bring the Constitution into avowed harmony with the Declaration of Independence." Preparing the ground for his next battle, he also reiterated the importance of guaranteeing all persons equality before the law, as that phrase "gives precision to the idea of human rights which is enunciated in our Declaration of Independence." Senator Henry Wilson of Massachusetts also argued for the necessity of annihilating the "last lingering vestiges of the slave system." When the Senate voted, two Democrats crossed party lines and joined the thirty-six Republicans in supporting the amendment.

Defeat loomed, however, in the House of Representatives, where Republicans outnumbered Democrats only 102 to 75. On June 15, 1864, the vote fell eleven short of the required two-thirds majority. The defeat in the House assured that the proposed amendment would be a key issue in the upcoming presidential and congressional elections. That Lincoln might be replaced was a real possibility. The bloody war continued to rage, and no sitting president had won reelection since Andrew Jackson in 1832.

THE ELECTION OF 1864

Lincoln would face opposition from a splinter group of Radical Republicans, including Wendell Phillips, and from the Democrats. Garrison, who had for so long opposed compromise, now staunchly defended Lincoln. Garrison no longer doubted Lincoln's personal commitment to permanently ending slavery and had become convinced of the efficacy of his tempered approach. "As the stream cannot rise higher than the fountain, so the President of the United States, amenable to public sentiment, could not, if he wished to do it, far transcend public sentiment in any direction," he wrote. On March 18, 1864, Garrison endorsed Lincoln's reelection in an editorial in *The Liberator*, stating, "We have advanced a quarter of a century in a single year."

But Phillips was implacable. When it became clear that the Republican Party would renominate Lincoln at its July convention, he became a proponent of a new party, the Radical Democracy Party, which met in May in Cleveland, Ohio, and nominated John Fremont for the presidency. Fremont had harbored resentment against Lincoln—and been a hero to many radical Republicans—ever since he issued his 1861 military decree freeing Missouri's slaves and been punished with loss of his command. The platform of the Radical Democracy Party called for a constitutional amendment to end slavery and permit black suffrage as well as for the confiscation and redistribution of land owned by wealthy Confederates. Governor Andrew and Frederick Douglass were among those who joined Phillips in supporting Fremont.

Hub of the Second Revolution

Garrison attended the Republican convention in Baltimore. Republicans renominated Lincoln and called for the pursuit of war until the Confederacy surrendered unconditionally. Seeking to attract "War Democrats" who supported that mission (rather than a negotiated end to the war), the Republicans changed their name to the National Unity Party and replaced Vice President Hannibal Hamlin with Andrew Johnson, a "War Democrat" from Tennessee, on the ticket. Seeking also to stem defections to Fremont, the Republican platform explicitly called for a constitutional amendment to end slavery:

> *Resolved, That as slavery was the cause, and now constitutes the strength of this Rebellion, and as it must be, always and everywhere, hostile to the principles of Republican Government, justice and the National safety demand its utter and complete extirpation from the soil of the Republic; and that…we are in favor, furthermore, of such an amendment to the Constitution.*

In his letter accepting the nomination, Lincoln broke his silence on the proposed Thirteenth Amendment, writing that "the resolutions of the convention, called the platform, are heartily approved." Shortly afterward, Garrison, whose metamorphosis from reviled outsider to moral hero was largely completed, went to Washington, D.C., where he met privately with the president. Lincoln shared that he had personally insisted that the Republican platform support a constitutional amendment ending slavery.

The Democratic convention, held in August, found the party badly divided between "War Democrats" and "Peace Democrats." War Democrats pledged to fight until the Union was restored but promised to manage the war effort more capably than Lincoln. Many of them also supported the Emancipation Proclamation, believing it a necessary instrument of military victory. Peace Democrats, known as "copperheads" by Republicans, who likened them to venomous snakes, sought a reconciliation with the Confederacy that would leave slavery intact. The divided party nominated War Democrat General George McClellan for the presidency but Peace Democrat George Pendleton as his running mate. The Democrats endorsed a "peace platform" that called for the cessation of hostilities "at the earliest practicable moment" and the restoration of states' rights "unimpaired." Boston flour merchant Samuel Bowdlear described the outcome to his former apprentice, Austin Clark Wellington. The Democrats, wrote Bowdlear, have "a war candidate [McClellan] standing on a peace platform. Mr. face-him-both-ways will have a hard time to keep on his platform."

While few doubted that the abolitionist stronghold of Massachusetts would cast its electoral votes for Lincoln, McClellan had support in Boston. The Irish community remained strongly in the Democratic column. Other Boston conservatives had rallied behind a possible McClellan candidacy soon after Lincoln removed him from command, and McClellan had spent nine days during January 1863 courting Boston's remaining "cotton Whigs." In reaction to the support shown McClellan by some upper-class Bostonians, wealthy Lincoln supporters founded the Union Club on Park Street. Article I of the new club's charter provided: "The condition of membership shall be unqualified support to the Constitution and Union of the United States and unwavering support of the federal government in efforts for the suppression of the Rebellion."

As the summer of 1864 drew to a close, prospects for Lincoln's reelection dimmed. The Union army had still not captured any of the Confederate strongholds of Richmond, Atlanta or Charleston. Frustration followed a military disaster in Petersburg, Virginia, where Union forces were engaged in a lengthy siege. An attempt to use explosives to blow a hole in Confederate lines ended up leaving Union soldiers trapped and defenseless in an enormous crater, resulting in nearly four thousand casualties. Adding to that setback, Confederate commander Jubal Early moved troops through the Shenandoah Valley and across the Potomac River into the District of Columbia before his daring plan to capture the capital was thwarted. Democrats claimed that Lincoln was an incompetent commander-in-chief. At the same time, radical Republicans became infuriated when Lincoln pocket-vetoed the Wade-Davis Bill, which would have required over 50 percent of voters (as opposed to the 10 percent Lincoln had proposed) to swear loyalty to the Unites States before a seceded state could be readmitted.

Lincoln's reelection prospects seemed so bleak that on August 23, he wrote a secret, sealed memorandum to his cabinet revealing his worry that he would not be reelected. This poignant memorandum pledged his cooperation with the president-elect to save the Union between the election and inauguration because the victor "will have secured his election on such ground that he can not possibly save it [the Union] afterwards."

Lincoln's electoral prospects dramatically improved on September 7, when General Sherman telegraphed, "Atlanta is ours and fairly won." On the heels of this key victory, Rear Admiral David Farragut ordered his men to "damn the torpedoes, full steam ahead" and led the navy to capture the important Confederate port of Mobile, Alabama. In the aftermath of these victories, Fremont abandoned his campaign. Though harshly condemning Lincoln's administration as a failure "politically, militarily, and financially," Fremont wrote that he was withdrawing to prevent the election of McClellan: "The policy of the Democratic Party signifies either separation, or reestablishment with Slavery…The Republican candidate on the contrary is pledged to the reestablishment of the Union without slavery; and however hesitating his policy may be, the pressure of his party will, we may hope, force him to it."

Phillips still refused to support Lincoln's reelection and announced, "I mean to agitate till I bayonet him and his party into justice." But nearly all of Boston's other prominent abolitionists supported Lincoln. Sumner admonished audiences that Republican unity "must be had at all hazards." John Rock likely expressed the views of many black Bostonians when he spoke at a National Convention of Colored Men in Syracuse, New York. Rock announced, "There are but two parties in the country today. The one headed by Lincoln is for Freedom and the Republic; and the other, by McClellan, is for Despotism and Slavery. There can be no middle ground in war." But Rock also stressed the need to plan a post-election strategy that would seek equal opportunities and equal rights. Douglass underscored that focus, arguing that ballots must follow bullets because "possession of that right [to vote] is the keystone to the arch of human liberty."

In the November election, Massachusetts favored Lincoln with 72.2 percent of the vote against McClellan's 27.8 percent. Andrew was elected to his fifth one-year term as governor. Lincoln's wide victory margin in Massachusetts was exceeded only in Vermont and the recently admitted Kansas. Overall, Lincoln received 55 percent of the popular vote. McClellan won only the states of Delaware, Kentucky, and New Jersey, although Lincoln's margin of victory was less than 5 percent in several states, including Connecticut, New York and Pennsylvania. The Republicans slightly increased their congressional majorities.

The Thirteenth Amendment Reprise

Garrison wrote that Lincoln's reelection made clear beyond doubt that the rebellion and slavery must "expire together and find the same ignominious grave." He said the next session of Congress should immediately reconsider the Thirteenth Amendment. But Lincoln decided not to wait for the new Congress. Soon after the election, he turned his focus to securing passage of the amendment in the House. He explained his rationale:

> *Although the present is the same Congress and nearly the same members…I venture to recommend the reconsideration and passage of the measure at the present session. Of course the abstract question is not changed; but an intervening election shows almost certainly that the next Congress will pass the measure if this does not. Hence there is only a question of time as to when the proposed amendment will go to the States for their action. And as it is to so go, at all events, may we not agree that the sooner the better?*

Lincoln also presumably chose to act because the end of the war appeared imminent, and he wanted to secure passage before the Confederacy surrendered. As it turned out, Lincoln would live for only a few more months, so it was fortunate that he turned his political skill and muscle to the passage of the Thirteenth Amendment. Steven Spielberg's acclaimed 2012 movie *Lincoln* portrayed some of the coaxing, threatening and horse trading required to secure the necessary votes for passage. On January 31, 1865, with the galleries full and the outcome uncertain even as voting began, the House of Representatives adopted the amendment with 119 voting in favor and 56 opposed. Lincoln's secretaries Hay and Nicolay described the moment when the amendment passed:

> *The members on the Republican side of the House instantly sprung to their feet, and, regardless of parliamentary rules, applauded with cheers and clapping of hands. The example was followed by the male spectators in the galleries, which were crowded to excess, who waved their hats and cheered loud and long, while the ladies, hundreds of whom were present, rose in their seats and waved their handkerchiefs.*

Although not legally required, Lincoln insisted on signing the amendment before it was sent to the states for ratification. Speaking extemporaneously to a celebratory crowd, he declared the amendment "a king's cure for all the evils." Lincoln also insisted on including returning Confederate states in the ratification process so that the future legitimacy of the amendment could never be disputed.

On February 4, black and white members of the antislavery community gathered to celebrate at Boston's Music Hall. Garrison announced:

> *At last, after eighty years of wandering and darkness, of cruelty and oppression, on a colossal scale…the nation, rising in the majesty of its moral power and political sovereignty, has decreed that Liberty shall be*

Hub of the Second Revolution

"proclaimed throughout the land, to all the inhabitants thereof" and that henceforth no such anomalous being as slaveholder or slave shall exist beneath the "stars and stripes."

His son, William Lloyd Garrison Jr., described the poignant moment when the many voices celebrated in song: "Nothing during the evening brought to my mind so clearly the magnitude of the act we celebrated, its deeply religious as well as moral significance, as [the singing of] 'Sound the loud timbrel o'er Egypt's dark sea, Jehovah has triumphed, His people are free.'"[121] On February 7, Massachusetts ratified the Thirteenth Amendment.

Also in February 1865, John Rock became the first black attorney admitted to practice before the Supreme Court of the United States, the same court that had only eight years earlier denied that even freed blacks could be citizens of the United States. It was, said *Harper's Weekly*, an "extraordinary reversal." Chief Justice Roger Taney, the author of the *Dred Scott* opinion, had died in October 1864, and President Lincoln had named radical Republican Salmon Chase as the new chief justice. Fittingly, Charles Sumner presented the formal one-sentence request to admit Rock to the Supreme Court. The *New York Times* observed, "The grave to bury the *Dred*

The triumphant entrance of the Fifty-fifth Regiment into Charleston, South Carolina, on February 21, 1865. *Courtesy of the Library of Congress.*

Scott decision was in that one sentence dug; and it yawned there, wide open, under the eyes of some of the judges who had participated in the judicial crime against democracy and humanity."

Lincoln delivered his second inaugural address on March 4, 1865, on the eve of victory and just five weeks before his assassination. He there stated unequivocally what Boston's abolitionists had always known: that slavery was the cause of the war.

> *One-eighth of the whole population were colored slaves, not distributed generally over the Union, but localized in the southern part of it. These slaves constituted a peculiar and powerful interest. All knew that this interest was somehow the cause of the war. To strengthen, perpetuate, and extend this interest was the object for which the insurgents would rend the Union.*

Richmond finally capitulated on April 3. On April 9, General Robert E. Lee surrendered at Appomattox Court House. News of the surrender brought Boston to a happy standstill. "Business, private and public griefs, all were forgotten and absorbed in the general rejoicing," wrote William Schouler, the state's adjutant general.[122]

A Final Confederate Prisoner

Following the South's surrender, Alexander Hamilton Stephens, the vice president of the Confederacy, was imprisoned at Fort Warren in Boston Harbor. Throughout the war, Fort Warren had been the most humane of Civil War prisons, with a death rate of substantially less than 1 percent. Other wartime prisoners did not fare as well: nearly 26,000 of approximately 215,000 imprisoned Confederate soldiers died in Northern prisons, and nearly 30,000 of approximately 194,000 imprisoned Union soldiers died in Southern prisons. The notorious Southern prison of Andersonville, Georgia, had a death rate of almost 30 percent—nearly 13,000 prisoners died of disease, starvation, malnutrition or neglect. Andersonville commander Captain Henry Wirz was the only Confederate officer executed for war crimes after the war ended.

While imprisoned off the coast of Boston, Stephens kept a journal of his experiences and recorded his thoughts about the causes of the war. In March 1861, he had given the "Cornerstone Speech," in which he clearly articulated that the foundation of the Confederacy lay upon slavery (see Chapter 8). But at Fort Warren, he took a different approach, outlining what would become known as the "lost cause" or states' rights view of the war. "[Constitutional liberty] could be better effected by maintenance of the principles of the ultimate, absolute sovereignty of the States," wrote Stephens. "The slavery question had but little influence with the masses." The "lost cause" view of the war would, regrettably, shape history books and school curricula for decades and minimize the roles of both slavery and Boston's courageous abolitionists.

Stephens applied for a pardon under the provisions of President Andrew Johnson's forgiving amnesty proclamation. When it was granted, he returned to Georgia in October 1865. Like many Confederate leaders, he again became a Southern leader; he was subsequently elected a U.S. congressman and senator as well as governor of Georgia. With other former Confederate leaders, he worked hard during the postwar years to fabricate a romantic vision of the Southern "way of life," which had "gone with the wind" as a result of the War of Northern Aggression.

The Assassination of Lincoln

Shortly after Lee's surrender at Appomattox Court House, a victory celebration took place at Fort Sumter. On April 14, Major Robert Anderson hoisted the United States flag—the very same one that had flown over Fort Sumter prior to his surrendering it four years earlier. Garrison attended as an honored guest. At a banquet that followed the ceremony, he said of Charleston, "She is smitten to the dust. She has been brought down from her pride of place." When thousands of freed slaves greeted him in Charleston, he wrote, "My reception was beyond all description enthusiastic, and my feelings were unutterable." Garrison also paid a visit to the cemetery where John C. Calhoun was buried. At the tomb of the man who had defended the philosophical righteousness of slavery, Garrison said, "Down into a deeper grave than this, slavery has gone, and for this there is no resurrection."

Lincoln was, of course, invited to the Fort Sumter ceremony but chose to remain in Washington, D.C. He and his wife sought some well-earned relaxation by attending a comedy, *Our American Cousin*, at Ford's Theatre. During the show, John Wilkes Booth, a famous actor and Confederate sympathizer, assassinated Abraham Lincoln as he sat in the presidential box. Patron James S. Knox gave this eyewitness account the next morning:

> *Just after the 3d Act, and before the scenes were shifted, a muffled pistol shot was heard, and a man sprang wildly from the national box, partially tearing down the flag, then shouting "sic semper tyrannis, the south is avenged" with brandished dagger rushed across the stage and disappeared. The whole theatre was paralyzed...The shrill cry of murder from Mrs. Lincoln first roused the horrified audience, and in an instant the uproar was terrible. The silence of death was broken by shouts of "kill him," "hang him" and strong men wept, and cursed, and tore the seats in the impotence of their anger, while Mrs. Lincoln, on her knees uttered shriek after shriek at the feet of the dying President.*

Garrison received news of Lincoln's murder as he prepared for the next leg of his journey, which would have taken him to Florida. He immediately planned his return to Boston. "We had no more heart for pleasure," he recalled. "The heavens seemed dark. Nothing was left for the hour, but God, and his immutable providence and his decrees."

Boston, too, plunged from relief and joy to horror and grief. Bostonians gathered at Faneuil Hall to express their bereavement. The Boston City Council expressed its great sorrow while praising Lincoln's freeing of the slaves, resolving, "We recognize especially his great wisdom and foresight in issuing his proclamation of Emancipation, which will entitle him to the gratitude of the lovers of liberty throughout the world in all future ages, and give him a place in his country's fame by the side of the immortal Washington."

Governor Andrew was among those who attended Lincoln's funeral at the White House, which was held on April 19, the anniversary of the Lexingtons of 1775 and 1861. Of freedom's latest martyr, Garrison said, "He has died that his country might live. From the lowest security he has risen to sublime altitude in the service of Freedom and Humanity." Sumner echoed this theme in a eulogy he delivered in Boston. Perhaps, he wondered, Lincoln's death had a divine purpose—"to put Emancipation beyond all mortal question. Perhaps it was the sacrificial consecration of those primal truths embodied in the birthday Declaration of the Republic, which he had so often vindicated, and for which he had announced his willingness to die."

Hub of the Second Revolution

Verily the World Moves

The Thirteenth Amendment became part of the U.S. Constitution on December 6, 1865, when it was ratified by twenty-seven states, three-quarters of the thirty-six states (including states of the former Confederacy).

The Return of the Colors to the Custody of the Commonwealth. Mural by Edward Simmons, 1902. *Courtesy of the Commonwealth of Massachusetts Art Commission.*

Garrison rejoiced, "Freedom is triumphant! We are all abolitionists, we are all loyalists, to the backbone."

Soon thereafter, on December 22, 1865, Governor Andrew and the citizens of Massachusetts honored those who had fought in the war. Presiding over a ceremony known as the Return of the Flags, Governor Andrew received the regimental flags—many in tatters—from surviving members of each Massachusetts regiment. Andrew promised to preserve these flags "amid all the vicissitudes of the future, as mementos of brave men and noble actions." Several of these flags are on display at the Massachusetts State House.

William Lloyd Garrison after the Civil War. *Used with permission of istock.com.*

Garrison published his final edition of *The Liberator* at the end of December. The nation faced enormous, divisive challenges over the future of former slaves and the governments of the seceded states. However, he decided to conclude his newspaper with the abolition of slavery, as that was "the object for which *The Liberator* was commenced." William Nell wrote an emotional farewell to *The Liberator* in which he observed that the events of the past thirty-five years had demonstrated that "verily the world moves."

The first stage of the Second American Revolution was complete. The city whose Patriot ancestors had planted the Liberty Tree had finally succeeded in spreading its seeds throughout the nation. But while the battle for liberty had been won, the one for equality was still pending.[123] Boston's abolitionists now turned their full attention to the fights against racism and for civil and political rights that lay immediately ahead. Here again, they would play leading roles in the ongoing effort to create a "more perfect union."

Notes

I provide citations only when necessary to give credit to those authors who compiled collections of primary sources or wrote secondary sources on which I relied. In general, I do not provide citations where I relied on my own primary source research, most of which was conducted by accessing speeches, letters and collections of primary source documents (including newspapers) in the public domain. See www.CivilWarBoston.org for more information.

Chapter 1

1. Handlin and Handlin, *Popular Sources of Political Authority*, 769, 830 (Hardwick and Braintree).
2. New York's gradual emancipation laws were passed in 1799 and 1817.
3. Mayer, *All on Fire*, 106.

Chapter 2

4. "Radical abolitionists" generally refers to those who sought an immediate end to both slavery and racism; they supported granting full political and civil rights to blacks.
5. Newman, *Transformation of American Abolitionism*, 147.

6. Bradley Newcomb Cumings Journal, October 21, 1835. This document is found in the Massachusetts Historical Society's online Civil War Object of the Month project.
7. Sklar, *Women's Rights*, 113.
8. Ibid., 29.
9. MassMoments.org, "Angela Grimké Addresses Legislature, February 21, 1838." http://www.massmoments.org/moment.cfm?mid=59.
10. Minardi, *Making Slavery History*, 80.

Chapter 3

11. Robboy and Robboy, *Lewis Hayden*, 592.
12. Ibid., 593.
13. Collison, *Shadrach Minkins*, 134.
14. Ibid., 136.
15. Remini, *Daniel Webster*, 696.
16. Reynolds, *Mightier Than the Sword*, 115.
17. Mayer, *All on Fire*, 437.
18. The quotes of Mary E. Blanchard are contained in her June 4, 1854 letter to Benjamin Seaver. This document is found in the Massachusetts Historical Society's online Civil War Object of the Month project.
19. Von Frank, *Trials of Anthony Burns*, 278.
20. Green, *Politics and America in Crisis*, 81.

Chapter 4

21. New York State Senate Judiciary Committee Report, quoted in Justice Stephen Breyer, "Guardian of the Constitution: The Counter Example of Dred Scott," New York Historical Society lecture, April 21, 2010. Available online.
22. Horton, *Bostonians*, 124; Kantrowitz, *More Than Freedom*, 248–49; Robboy and Robboy, *Lewis Hayden*, 608.
23. Stauffer, *Tribunal*, 80, 118 (the *Boston Courier* and Douglass).
24. Ibid., 105, 113–14, 162 (Emerson, Thoreau, Garrison). A slave coffle is a line of slaves chained together.
25. Ware, *Public Opinion*, 27.

26. Adam Goodheart, "The Abolitionist's Epiphany," in *New York Times: Disunion* (November 6, 2010).
27. Hamrogue, "John A. Andrew," 46.
28. Schouler, *History*, vol. 1, p. 20.
29. MassMoments.org, "Sixth Massachusetts Volunteer Regiment Organized, January 21, 1861." http://www.massmoments.org/moment.cfm?mid=26.
30. Ware, *Public Opinion*, 70–71.
31. Ibid., 69.

Chapter 5

32. This section is based on the letters of Paul Joseph Revere contained in the collection of the Massachusetts Historical Society. Secondary sources consulted include Miller, *Harvard's Civil War* and Higginson, *Harvard Memorial Biographies*.
33. Miller, *Harvard's Civil War*, 21.
34. Lepore, "How Longfellow Woke the Dead."
35. Letter from Caspar Crowninshield to his mother, October 22, 1861. This document is found in the Massachusetts Historical Society's online Civil War Object of the Month project.
36. Miller, *Harvard's Civil War*, 28.
37. Ibid., 274.
38. This section is drawn from the voluminous correspondence between Austin Clark Wellington and Samuel Bowdlear that is preserved in the Special Collections of the Boston Public Library. The following letters are quoted: December 3, 1862; January 22, 1863; June 25, 1863; June 28, 1863; July 29, 1864; and December 18, 1864.
39. Correspondence of Brenda Fohlmeister with the author.
40. White, *Oliver Wendell Holmes Jr.*, 24. This section is based on Holmes's letters published in Howe, *Touched with Fire*. The quotations are found on pages 13, 18, 64, 73, 79, 80 and 92.
41. Menand, *Metaphysical Club*, 4.
42. This section is based on Chase's letters published in Collier and Collier, *Yours for the Union*. The quotations are found on pages 10, 28, 40, 91, 104, 153, 180, 189, 292, 374, 375 and 377.
43. Holmes, "In Our Youth Our Hearts Were Touched with Fire." Speech delivered on May 30, 1884, in Keene, New Hampshire.

Chapter 6

44. Even early histories of the woman suffrage movement in Massachusetts explicitly referenced Abigail Adams's famous letter. For example, see Robinson, *Massachusetts*, 7–8.
45. DuBois, *Feminism and Suffrage*, 33.
46. Massey, *Women in the Civil War*, 339.
47. Primary sources relied on are Stewart's *Religion and the Pure Principles of Morality: The Sure Foundation on Which We Must Build* and her four Boston speeches, all available online and reprinted in Richardson, *Maria W. Stewart*. Secondary sources consulted include Richardson, *Maria W. Stewart*; Hine, *Black Women in America*; and the website of the Boston African American National Historic Park.
48. Richardson, *Maria W. Stewart*, 89–90.
49. Primary sources relied on include Child's published writings and letters, many of which are available online. Secondary sources consulted include Clifford, *Crusader for Freedom* and Karcher, *A Lydia Maria Child Reader*.
50. Clifford, *Crusader for Freedom*, 229.
51. Primary sources relied on include letters available online or contained in Lasser, *Friends and Sisters* and Massachusetts Humanities Curriculum, *Making the World Better: The Struggle for Equality in 19th Century America*. Secondary sources consulted include Berenson, "Torn Asunder"; Million, *Woman's Voice*; Kerr, *Lucy Stone*; and the website of the Worcester Women's History Project.
52. Million, *Woman's Voice*, 93.
53. This section is based on Berenson, "Torn Asunder."
54. Primary sources relied on include documents Massachusetts Humanities Curriculum, *Making the World Better*. Secondary sources consulted include Yee, *Black Women Abolitionists*; Richardson, *Sarah Parker Remond*; and Porter, *Sarah Parker Remond*.
55. Yee, *Black Women Abolitionists*, 125.
56. Primary sources relied on are Alcott's journal, letters and *Hospital Sketches*, as well as documents contained in Myerson, *Selected Letters*.
57. Myerson, *Selected Letters*, 245–46.
58. Sources consulted include Giesberg, *Civil War Sisterhood*; Cheney, *Memoirs*; and Ginzberg, *Women*.
59. Cheney, *Memoirs*, 16.
60. Giesberg, *Civil War Sisterhood*, 154.

Chapter 7

61. Oxx, *Nativist Movement*, 37.
62. O'Connor, *Civil War Boston*, 22.
63. *The Pilot*'s strong influence on Boston's Irish is widely accepted by historians of the era. For example, see O'Connor, *Civil War Boston*; Samito, *Becoming American Under Fire*; Walsh, "*Boston Pilot*." Unless otherwise noted, references to *The Pilot* are based on issues in the library of Boston College. Where a quotation to *The Pilot* is contained in a secondary source, it is so noted.
64. Baum, *Civil War Party System*, 49.
65. Walsh, "*Boston Pilot*," 151.
66. Baum, *Civil War Party System*, 91.
67. Macnamara, *History of the Ninth Regiment*, 23–24.
68. O'Connor, *Civil War Boston*, 76.
69. Macnamara, *History of the Ninth Regiment*, 123–24.
70. Samito, *Commanding Boston's Irish Ninth*, xiii–xiv.
71. Kohl, *Irish Green and Union Blue*, 43.
72. Macnamara, *History of the Ninth Regiment*, 278–79; Barnard, *Campaigning*, 89.
73. Kohl, *Irish Green and Union Blue*, 79–80. Welsh would be mortally wounded at the Battle of Spotsylvania in May 1864.
74. Samito, *Becoming American Under Fire*, 106
75. Walsh, "*Boston Pilot* Reports," 15.
76. Samito, *Commanding Boston's Irish Ninth*, 163.
77. Kohl, *Irish Green and Union Blue*, 62.
78. Ibid., 62, 65.
79. Frederic Lincoln, a Republican, was elected mayor in 1862.
80. Kelly, "Ambiguous Loyalties," 200.
81. Kohl, *Irish Green and Union Blue*, 110, 114.
82. Anbinder, "Which Poor Man's Fight?" 349–50.
83. Walsh, "*Boston Pilot*," 174.
84. Baum, *Civil War Party System*, 95.

Chapter 8

85. McPherson, *Struggle for Equality*, 82.
86. Mayer, *All on Fire*, 527.

87. Stossel, "Battle Hymn of the Republic," *The Atlantic*, September 18, 2001.
88. Stauffer and Soskis, *Battle Hymn of the Republic*, 86–91.
89. Goodwin, *Team of Rivals*, 468
90. Mayer, *All on Fire*, 541
91. Lucy Larcom Diary, August 21, 1861. This document is found in the Massachusetts Historical Society's online Civil War Object of the Month project. Larcom was a poet, editor and abolitionist.
92. To Lincoln's utter dismay, General George McClellan failed to pursue Lee's army and permitted its retreat to Virginia.
93. Hamrogue, "John Andrew," 162.
94. Guelzo, *Lincoln's Emancipation Proclamation*, 124.
95. Reynolds, *Mightier Than the Sword*, ix.
96. Wesley, *William Cooper Nell*, 633–34.
97. Masur, *Lincoln's Hundred Days*, 211 (Chapman and Phillips).

Chapter 9

98. The First South Carolina Volunteers, composed of freed or escaped slaves and organized in November 1862, was the first Union army regiment of black soldiers. Massachusetts abolitionist Thomas Wentworth Higginson led that regiment.
99. Black men were allowed to enlist in the much smaller U.S. Navy. Joseph Hayden, the son of Lewis Hayden, was among those who joined the navy. Also joining the navy was Lewis Latimer, the son of self-emancipated slave George Latimer.
100. Kantrowitz, *More Than Freedom*, 277.
101. "Fire and Thunder: Massachusetts Blacks in the Civil War," Commonwealth Museum Exhibit (2007). The requirement that militiamen be white was not stricken from the Massachusetts militia law until 1863.
102. Miller, *Harvard's Civil War*, 46.
103. Duncan, *Blue-Eyed Child of Fortune*, 286.
104. 1860 U.S. census. The census gives the total Massachusetts population as over 1.1 million.
105. Cox, *Undying Glory*, 25. Thomas Sims, who had been returned to slavery from Boston in 1851, was among the recruiters. Sims had escaped from slavery soon after the war began.
106. Adams, *On the Altar of Freedom*, 9.

107. Photos of this monument appear in Berenson, *Walking Tours of Civil War Boston*.
108. Duncan, *Blue-Eyed Child of Fortune*, 343.
109. Adams, *On the Altar of Freedom*, 38.
110. Duncan, *Blue-Eyed Child of Fortune*, 384–85.
111. Emilio, *A Brave Black Regiment*, 80.
112. Carney's actions were the first of a black soldier recognized with this honor. However, he was not honored until 1900. Peter Drummey of the Massachusetts Historical Society supplied me with the date of Carney's promotion.
113. Trudeau, *Voices of the 55th*, 165.
114. CNN.com, "President Clinton Awards Medals of Honor to Corporal Andrew Jackson Smith and President Teddy Roosevelt, January 16, 2001." http://edition.cnn.com/TRANSCRIPTS/0101/16/se.04.html.
115. Peter Drummey of the Massachusetts Historical Society clarified when the men of the Fifth Cavalry were mounted.
116. Adams, *On the Altar of Freedom*, 120.
117. Trudeau, *Voices of the 55th*, 117.
118. Yacovone, *A Voice of Thunder*, 277.
119. Trudeau, *Voices of the 55th*, 229.

Chapter 10

120. This 1862 Act was itself based on the language of the Northwest Ordinance of 1787. Equal protection of the laws and suffrage would not be addressed until the Fourteenth and Fifteenth Amendments.
121. McPherson, *Negro's Civil War*, 52–53.
122. Schouler, *History of Massachusetts*, 623–24.
123. This sentence paraphrases a sentence in Sumner's eulogy for Lincoln.

Bibliography

My research relied heavily on primary sources. Many of these items were accessed online at publicly accessible websites, including the Library of Congress, the Massachusetts Historical Society, the Gilder Lehrman Society, Google Books and Project Gutenberg (for published collections of speeches in the public domain), newspaper archives and many others. Other primary sources are located in the collections of libraries, including the Boston College Library (*The Pilot* newspaper), the Boston Public Library, the Massachusetts Historical Society and the Schlesinger Library. The list below includes published collections of primary source material and secondary sources that were especially useful to the author. A full bibliography is available at www.CivilWarBoston.org.

Adams, Virginia, ed. *On the Altar of Freedom: A Black Soldier's Civil War Letters from the Front*. Amherst: University of Massachusetts Press, 1991.
Anbinder, Tyler. *Nativism and Slavery: The Northern Know Nothings and the Politics of the 1850s*. Oxford, UK: Oxford University Press, 1992.
The Atlantic. *The Civil War: Special Commemorative Issue*. Washington, D.C.: The Atlantic, 2011.
Barnard, Sandy, ed. *Campaigning with the Irish Brigade: Private John Ryan, 28th Massachusetts*. N.p.: AST Press, 2001.
Baum, Dale. *The Civil War Party System: The Case of Massachusetts, 1848–1876*. Chapel Hill: University of North Carolina Press, 2010.

Bibliography

Berenson, Alice F. "Torn Asunder: The Woman Suffrage Movement Divides over the Primary of Black or Woman Suffrage." Unpublished, 2011.

Berenson, Barbara. *Walking Tours of Civil War Boston: Hub of Abolitionism*. 2nd ed. Boston: The Freedom Trail Foundation, 2014.

Bowdlear, Samuel G., and Austin C. Wellington. "Correspondence, 1862–1865." Boston Public Library Collections.

Cain, William E., ed. *William Lloyd Garrison and the Fight Against Slavery: Selections from* The Liberator. New York: Bedford/St. Martin's, 1995.

Cheney, Ednah Dow Littlehale. *Memoirs of Lucretia Crocker and Abby W. May*. Prepared for private circulation in 1893.

Clifford, Deborah Pickman. *Crusader for Freedom: A Life of Lydia Maria Child*. Boston: Beacon Press, 1992.

Collier, John S., and Bonnie B. Collier. *Yours for the Union: The Civil War Letters of John W. Chase, First Massachusetts Light Artillery*. New York: Fordham University Press, 2004.

Collison, Gary. *Shadrach Minkins: From Fugitive Slave to Citizen*. Cambridge, MA: Harvard University Press, 1997.

Cox, Clinton. *Undying Glory: The Story of the Massachusetts 54th Regiment*. New York: Scholastic Inc., 1991.

Dhalle, Catherine. "History of the 55th Massachusetts Volunteer Infantry." *Lest We Forget* 3, no. 2 (April 1995).

Donald, David. *Charles Sumner and the Coming of the Civil War*. New York: Alfred A. Knopf, 1974.

DuBois, Ellen Carol. *Feminism and Suffrage: The Emergence of an Independent Women's Movement in America*. New York: Cornell University Press, 1999.

Duncan, Russell, ed. *Blue-Eyed Child of Fortune: The Civil War Letters of Colonel Robert Gould Shaw*. Athens: University of Georgia Press, 1992.

Emilio, Luis. *A Brave Black Regiment: The History of the 54th Massachusetts, 1863–1865*. Revised ed. New York: Da Capo Press, 1995.

Flood, Charles Bracelon. *1864: Lincoln at the Gates of History*. New York: Simon & Schuster, 2009.

Foner, Eric. *The Fiery Trial: Abraham Lincoln and American Slavery*. New York: W.W. Norton, 2010.

Fradin, Judith Bloom, and Dennis Brindell Fradin. *5,000 Miles to Freedom: Ellen and William Craft's Flight from Slavery*. Washington, D.C.: National Geographic, 2006.

Giesberg, Judith Ann. *Civil War Sisterhood: The U.S. Sanitary Commission and Women's Politics in Transition*. Boston: Northeastern University Press, 1990.

Bibliography

Goodheart, Adam. *1861: The Civil War Awakening*. New York: Alfred A. Knopf, 2011.

Goodwin, Doris Kearns. *Team of Rivals: The Political Genius of Abraham Lincoln*. New York: Simon & Schuster, 2005.

Green, Michael S. *Politics and America in Crisis: The Coming of the Civil War*. Santa Barbara, CA: Praeger, 2010.

Guelzo, Allen G. *Lincoln's Emancipation Proclamation: The End of Slavery in America*. New York: Simon & Schuster, 2004.

Hamrogue, John M. "John A. Andrew: Abolitionist Governor, 1861–1865." PhD dissertation, Fordham University, 1974.

Handlin, Oscar, and Mary Handlin. *The Popular Sources of Political Authority: Documents on the Massachusetts Constitution of 1780*. Cambridge, MA: Harvard University Press, 1966.

Higginson, Thomas Wentworth. *Harvard Memorial Biographies*. Cambridge, MA: Sever and Francis, 1866.

Hinks, Peter P., ed. *David Walker's Appeal to the Coloured Citizens of the World*. Park, PA: Penn State University Press, 2000. (Originally published as David Walker's Appeal in four articles, 1829.)

Horton, James Oliver, and Lois E. Black Horton. *Bostonians: Family Life and Community Struggle in the Antebellum North*. New York: Holmes & Meier, 1979.

Horwitz, Tony. *Midnight Rising: John Brown and the Raid that Sparked the Civil War*. New York: Henry Holt & Co., 2011.

Howe, Mark De Wolfe, ed. *Touched with Fire: The Civil War Letters and Diary of Oliver Wendell Holmes Jr*. New York: Fordham University Press, 2000.

Jacobs, Donald M., ed. *Courage and Conscience: Black and White Abolitionists in Boston*. Bloomington: Indiana University Press, 1993.

Jacobs, Harriet. *Incidents in the Life of a Slave Girl*. Mineola, NY: Dover Publications Inc., 2001.

Kantrowitz, Stephen. *More Than Freedom: Fighting for Black Citizenship in a White Republic, 1829–1889*. New York: Penguin Press, 2012.

Karcher, Carolyn L., ed. *A Lydia Maria Child Reader*. Durham, NC: Duke University Press, 1997.

Kelley, Brian. "Ambiguous Loyalties: The Boston Irish, Slavery, and the Civil War." *Historical Journal of Massachusetts* (1996).

Kerr, Andrea Moore. *Lucy Stone: Speaking Out for Equality*. New Brunswick, NJ: Rutgers University Press, 1992.

Kohl, Richard, and Margaret Richard. *Irish Green and Union Blue: The Civil War Letters of Peter Welsh*. New York: Fordham University Press, 1986.

Lepore, Jill. "How Longfellow Woke the Dead." *American Scholar* (Spring 2011).

Bibliography

Lerner, Gerder. *The Grimké Sisters from South Carolina: Pioneers for Women's Rights and Abolition*. Boston: Houghton Mifflin, 1967.

Macnamara, Daniel George. *The History of the Ninth Regiment: Massachusetts Volunteer Infantry, June 1861–June 1864*. New York: Fordham University Press, 2000.

Masur, Louis P. *Lincoln's Hundred Days*. Cambridge, MA: Harvard University Press, 2012.

Mayer, Henry. *All on Fire: William Lloyd Garrison and the Abolition of Slavery*. New York: W.W. Norton & Co., 1998.

McClymer, John F. *This High and Holy Moment: The First National Woman's Rights Convention, Worcester, 1850*. New York: Harcourt Brace & Co., 1999.

McPherson, James. *The Struggle for Equality: Abolitionists and the Negro in the Civil War and Reconstruction*. Princeton, NJ: Princeton University Press, 1964.

Meltzer, Milton, and Patricia Holland. *Lydia Maria Child: Selected Letters, 1817–1880*. Amherst: University of Massachusetts Press, 1982.

Menand, Louis. *The Metaphysical Club*. New York: Farrar, Straus and Girous, 2001.

Miller, Richard F. *Harvard's Civil War: A History of the Twentieth Massachusetts Volunteer Infantry*. Lebanon, NH: University Press of New England, 2005.

Million, Joelle. *Woman's Voice, Woman's Place: Lucy Stone and the Birth of the Woman's Rights Movement*. Westport, CT: Praeger, 2003.

Minardi, Margot. *Making Slavery History: Abolition and the Politics of Memory in Massachusetts*. Oxford, UK: Oxford University Press, 2010.

Mulkern, John R. *The Know Nothing Party in Massachusetts: The Rise and Fall of a People's Movement*. Boston: Northeastern University Press, 1990.

Myerson, Joel, and Daniel Shealy. *Selected Letters of Louisa May Alcott*. Athens: University of Georgia Press, 1995.

Newman, Richard S. *The Transformation of American Abolitionism: Fighting Slavery in the Early Republic*. Chapel Hill: University of North Carolina Press, 2002.

O'Connor, Thomas H. *Civil War Boston: Home Front and Battlefield*. Boston: Northeastern University Press, 1997.

Oxx, Katie. *The Nativist Movement in America: Religious Conflict in the Nineteenth Century*. New York: Routledge, 2013.

Porter, Dorothy B. "Sarah Parker Remond: Abolitionist and Physician." *Journal of Negro History* 20, no. 3 (July 1935).

Reisen, Harriet. *Louisa May Alcott: The Woman Behind* Little Women. New York: Picador, 2010.

Remini, Robert. *Daniel Webster: The Man and His Time*. New York: W.W. Norton & Co., 1997.

Bibliography

Reynolds, David S. *Mightier Than the Sword:* Uncle Tom's Cabin *and the Battle for America*. New York: W.W. Norton and Co., 2011.

Richardson, Marilyn. *Maria W. Stewart, America's First Black Woman Political Writer: Essays and Speeches*. Bloomington: Indiana University Press, 1987.

———. "Sarah Parker Remond: A Daughter of Salem, Massachusetts." http://sarahparkerremond.wordpress.com.

Robboy, Stanley J., and Anita W. Robboy. "Lewis Hayden: From Fugitive Slave to Statesman." *New England Quarterly* 46, no. 4 (December 1973): 591–613.

Samito, Christian G. *Becoming American Under Fire: Irish Americans, African Americans, and the Politics of Citizenship During the Civil War Era*. Ithaca, NY: Cornell University Press, 2009.

Samito, Christian G., ed. *Commanding Boston's Irish Ninth: The Civil War Letters of Colonel Patrick Guiney*. New York: Fordham University Press, 1998.

Schmidt, Jay. *Fort Warren: New England's Most Historic Civil War Site*. Amherst, NH: UBT Press, 2003.

Schouler, William A. *History of Massachusetts in the Civil War*. Boston: E.P Dutton & Co., 1868.

Sklar, Kathryn Kish. *Women's Rights Emerges within the Antislavery Movement, 1830–1870*. New York: Bedford, 2000.

Stauffer, John, and Benjamin Soskis. *Battle Hymn of the Republic: A Biography of the Song That Marches On*. Oxford, UK: Oxford University Press, 2013.

———. *Giants: The Parallel Lives of Frederick Douglass and Abraham Lincoln*. New York: Twelve Books, 2008.

Stauffer, John, and Zoe Trodd, eds. *The Tribunal: Responses to John Brown and the Harpers Ferry Raid*. Cambridge, MA: Harvard University Press, 2012.

Stewart, James Brewer. *Wendell Phillips: Liberty's Hero*. Baton Rouge: Louisiana State University Press, 1986.

Tsesis, Alexander. *The Thirteenth Amendment and American Freedom*. New York: New York University Press, 2004.

Trudeau, Noah Andre. *Voices of the 55th: Letters from the 55th Massachusetts Volunteers, 1861–1865*. Dayton, OH: Morningside House Inc., 1996.

Von Drehle, David. *Rise to Greatness: Abraham Lincoln and America's Most Perilous Year*. New York: Henry Holt & Co., 2012.

Von Frank, Albert J. *The Trials of Anthony Burns: Freedom and Slavery in Emerson's Boston*. Cambridge, MA: Harvard University Press, 1998.

Vorenberg, Michael. *Final Freedom: The Civil War, the Abolition of Slavery, and the Thirteenth Amendment*. Cambridge, UK: Cambridge University Press, 2001.

Walsh, Francis R. "The *Boston Pilot*: A Newspaper for the Irish Immigrant, 1829–1908." Dissertation, Boston University, 1968.

Bibliography

———. "The *Boston Pilot* Reports the Civil War." *Historical Journal of Massachusetts* 5 (1981).

Ware, Edith Ellen. "Public Opinion in Massachusetts During the Civil War and Reconstruction." Dissertation, Columbia University, 1916.

Waugh, John C. *On the Brink of Civil War: The Compromise of 1850 and How it Changed the Course of American History*. Wilmington, DE: Scholarly Resources Inc., 2003.

———. *Reelecting Lincoln: The Battle for the 1864 Presidency*. New York: Crown Publishers Inc., 1997.

Wesley, Dorothy Porter, and Constance Porter Uzelac, ed. *William Cooper Nell: Nineteenth-Century African American Abolitionist, Historian, Integrationist; Selected Writings, 1832–1874*. Baltimore, MD: Black Classic Press, 2002.

White, G. Edward. *Oliver Wendell Holmes Jr*. Oxford, UK: Oxford University Press, 2006.

Widmer, Ted, ed., *The* New York Times: *Disunion: Modern Historians Revisit and Reconsider the Civil War from Lincoln's Election to the Emancipation Proclamation*. New York: Black Dog & Leventhal, 2013.

Yacovone, Donald, ed. *A Voice of Thunder: The Civil War Letters of George E. Stephens*. Chicago: University of Illinois Press, 1997.

———. *Freedom's Journey: African American Voices of the Civil War*. Chicago: Lawrence Hill Books, 2004.

Yee, Shirley J. *Black Women Abolitionists: A Study in Activism*. Knoxville: University of Tennessee Press, 1993.

Index

A

Adams, Abigail 12, 97
Adams, Charles Francis 38, 154, 156
Adams, John 12, 13, 38
Adams, John Quincy 23, 38, 136
African Meeting House 17, 21, 25, 35, 101, 148
Alcott, Louisa May 100, 109, 110, 111
American Woman Suffrage Association 100, 107, 113
Andrew, John Albion 73, 75, 76, 79, 117, 118, 119, 123, 138, 144, 145, 146, 148, 149, 154, 156, 157, 162, 170, 172
Anthony, Susan B. 106, 161
Antietam 86, 90, 93, 137, 145
Atlantic Monthly, The 68, 75, 84

B

"Battle Hymn of the Republic" 71, 107, 133, 135
Bloody Kansas 62, 63, 64
Boston Female Anti-Slavery Society 27, 28, 34
Bowdlear, Samuel 87, 88, 149, 163
Brown, John 70, 71, 72, 74, 75, 104, 110, 117, 133, 135, 149
Burns, Anthony 54, 57, 58, 59, 60, 62, 116, 143
Butler, Benjamin 129

C

Calhoun, John 24, 169
Carney, William Harvey 153
Cass, Thomas 116, 118, 120
Chancellorsville 91, 92, 93, 120, 123
Chapman, Maria Weston 28, 31, 141
Chase, John 92, 93, 95
Child, Lydia Maria 23, 98, 99, 102, 104, 136, 137
Clay, Henry 41
colonization 19, 21, 23, 101, 103, 137, 140
Compromise of 1820 16, 38, 41, 56, 57, 67
Compromise of 1850 44, 45, 49, 68, 129
Constitutional Union Party 74
Craft, Ellen and William 47, 48, 49, 50, 104, 109
Crispus Attucks Day 69, 72
Curtis, Benjamin Robbins 68

Index

D

Davis, Jefferson 76
Declaration of Independence 11, 13, 15, 18, 19, 23, 60, 66, 98, 128, 133, 161
Democratic Party 38, 39, 62, 73, 93, 117, 124, 165
disunion 67, 73, 79, 128
Dix, Dorothea 110, 112
Donahoe, Patrick 116, 117, 118, 119
Douglass, Frederick 32, 33, 34, 60, 72, 104, 106, 107, 108, 138, 139, 141, 144, 148, 152, 153, 162, 165
Douglas, Stephen A. 45, 73
Dred Scott case 63, 67, 68, 69, 73, 167, 168

E

Emancipation Proclamation 83, 92, 93, 121, 135, 136, 137, 138, 139, 140, 141, 143, 145, 159, 160, 163
Emerson, Ralph Waldo 45, 66, 68, 72, 139
Everett, Edward 74, 79

F

Faneuil Hall 21, 27, 29, 30, 34, 57, 58, 70, 77, 107, 170
Fifth Cavalry 154, 156
Fifty-fifth Regiment 154, 157
Fifty-fourth Regiment 143, 145, 148, 149, 151, 153, 154
Fillmore, Millard 39, 45, 49, 51, 54, 66
Fort Sumter 77, 79, 151, 169
Fort Wagner 151, 152, 153, 154, 157
Fort Warren 131, 132, 133, 168, 169
Fredericksburg 91, 92, 93, 120, 123
Freeman, Elizabeth 13
Free Soil Party 37, 38, 39, 45, 54, 61, 116, 156
Fremont, John C. 66, 117, 130, 131, 139, 162, 163, 164, 165
Fugitive Slave Act of 1850 45

G

Garrison, William Lloyd 11, 14, 18, 19, 21, 22, 23, 24, 25, 28, 29, 31, 33, 36, 37, 46, 59, 60, 66, 67, 72, 76, 79, 97, 98, 100, 102, 103, 104, 107, 110, 127, 128, 131, 133, 137, 141, 149, 154, 159, 162, 163, 165, 166, 167, 169, 170, 172
Gettysburg 86, 92, 120, 151, 160
Gooding, James Henry 148, 151, 154, 156, 157
Great Awakening 16, 27, 97
Greeley, Horace 62, 104, 136
Grimes, Leonard 52, 58, 59, 69, 148, 149
Grimké, Sarah and Angelina 29, 30, 31, 32, 55, 98, 102

H

Harpers Ferry 70, 71, 72, 74, 104, 117, 133, 185
Hayden, Lewis 45, 46, 47, 49, 51, 52, 58, 62, 71, 143, 144, 148
Hayne, Robert 24
Higginson, Thomas Wentworth 67, 71
Holmes, Oliver Wendell, Jr. 89, 90, 91, 95
Holmes, Oliver Wendell, Sr. 68, 139
Howe, Julia Ward 107, 133

I

Irish in Boston 58, 60, 61, 62, 81, 83, 115, 116, 117, 118, 119, 120, 121, 123, 124, 125, 164

K

Kansas-Nebraska Act 54, 57, 59, 60, 62, 63, 64, 67, 71, 104, 117
Know Nothing Party 60, 61, 62, 66, 117, 121, 124

L

Latimer, George 34, 35, 37

Index

Lawrence, Amos A. 59, 65
League of Freedom 45, 49
Lexington of 1861 63, 77
Liberator, The 11, 18, 21, 22, 23, 25, 29, 31, 33, 36, 49, 59, 97, 128, 141, 159, 172
Liberty Party 37, 38
Lincoln, Abraham 39, 56, 63, 68, 71, 73, 74, 75, 117, 119, 123, 124, 127, 130, 132, 136, 137, 138, 140, 156, 157, 160, 165, 166, 167, 168, 170
Longfellow, Henry Wadsworth 68, 84, 139
Lovejoy, Elijah 29, 71
Lowell, Francis Cabot 16

M

Massachusetts General Colored Association 17, 27, 35
May, Abigail Williams 100, 111, 112, 113
May, Samuel Joseph 21, 109, 111
McClellan, George 93, 119, 124, 163, 164, 165
Minkins, Shadrach 50, 51
Morris, Robert 35, 36, 45, 51, 58, 143, 148

N

National Woman Suffrage Association 107
Nell, William Cooper 35, 36, 38, 45, 62, 69, 108, 139, 141, 148, 172
New England Anti-Slavery Society 25, 27, 35, 36, 101, 106
Nineteenth Amendment 113
Ninth Regiment 118, 119, 120
Northup, Solomon 56

P

Parker, Theodore 45, 46, 49, 51, 57, 71, 109, 116

Paul, Thomas 21
Phillips, Wendell 29, 30, 33, 46, 47, 57, 60, 67, 75, 79, 90, 105, 107, 109, 127, 128, 136, 141, 156, 160, 162, 165
Pierce, Franklin 57
Pilot, The 116, 117, 118, 121, 123, 124

R

Remond, Charles Lenox 108
Remond, Sarah Parker 100, 102, 108, 109
Republican Party 38, 61, 62, 63, 66, 67, 68, 71, 73, 117, 120, 124, 162
Revere, Paul Joseph 83, 84, 85, 86, 95, 175
Roberts v. City of Boston 37, 54, 61
Rock, John 69, 71, 72, 139, 143, 148, 165, 167

S

Sanitary Commission 112
Schouler, William 124, 168
secession 44, 63, 67, 70, 72, 74, 75, 76, 118, 128, 129, 130
Sewall, Samuel E. 21, 109
Seward, William H. 74
Shaw, Lemuel 34, 37, 52, 61
Shaw, Robert Gould 145, 146, 149, 151, 157
Sims, Thomas 51, 52, 54, 138, 143
Sixth Massachusetts Volunteer Militia 77, 78
Smith, Andrew Jackson 154
Snowden, Samuel 21
Stanton, Elizabeth Cady 106
Stephens, Alexander Hamilton 76, 128, 168, 169
Stewart, Maria 23, 99, 100, 101, 102
Stone, Lucy 99, 102, 105, 106, 107, 113, 161
Stowe, Harriet Beecher 54, 56, 116, 138
St. Patrick's Day 120

189

Index

Sumner, Charles 35, 36, 37, 54, 57, 60, 62, 63, 64, 65, 66, 74, 79, 84, 104, 128, 129, 132, 138, 139, 141, 145, 160, 161, 165, 167, 170

T

Taylor, Zachary 39
Thirteenth Amendment 159, 160, 161, 163, 165, 166, 167, 171
Thoreau, Henry David 60, 72
Tremont Temple Baptist Church 39, 57, 58, 75, 139
Trent affair 131
Twelfth Baptist Church 47, 52, 57, 58, 69
Twentieth Regiment 83, 84, 86, 90
Twenty-eighth Regiment 119

U

Uncle Tom's Cabin 54, 55, 56, 59
Union Club 164
U.S. Constitution 15, 23, 34, 52, 60, 97, 113, 171

V

Van Buren, Martin 38
Vigilance Committee 46, 47, 49, 52

W

Walker, David 14, 15, 17, 18, 19, 21
Walker, Quock 14
Webster, Daniel 23, 24, 39, 44, 45, 47, 51, 54, 68, 74, 141
Wellington, Austin Clark 86, 87, 88, 89, 95, 163
Welsh, Peter 120, 121, 123, 124
Wheatley, Phillis 12, 104
Whig Party 38, 39, 66

About the Author

Barbara F. Berenson is the author of *Walking Tours of Civil War Boston: Hub of Abolitionism* (2011, 2nd ed. 2014) and co-editor of *Breaking Barriers: The Unfinished Story of Women Lawyers and Judges in Massachusetts* (2012). A graduate of Harvard College and Harvard Law School, Barbara works as a senior attorney at the Massachusetts Supreme Judicial Court.

Visit us at
www.historypress.net

This title is also available as an e-book